The Four Steps of Love

The Four Steps of Love

FIONA GARDNER

DARTON·LONGMAN+TODD

First published in Great Britain in 2007 by
Darton, Longman and Todd Ltd
1 Spencer Court
140–142 Wandsworth High Street
London SW18 4JJ

ISBN–10   0–232–52716–4
ISBN–13   978–0–232–52716–2

A catalogue record for this book is available
from the British Library.

Designed and produced by Sandie Boccacci
Phototypeset in 10.5/13.75pt Palatino
Printed and bound in Great Britain by
Page Bros, Norwich, Norfolk

For Peter

CONTENTS

ACKNOWLEDGEMENTS

＞＜

THANK YOU TO THE COMMUNITY AT Downside Abbey for access to their excellent library. I would also like to thank the Community of St Francis at Compton Durville, Somerset, for their hospitality during retreats over the last few years. I am particularly grateful to Sr Carol of the Community of the Holy Name for her continuing wisdom and guidance and for introducing me to the writings of Abbé de Tourville.

I would like to acknowledge friends and colleagues in my work in the Diocese of Bath and Wells, and the clergy of St John the Baptist, Midsomer Norton.

Thank you to Sheila Davies for her guidance on Mary, and to Alex Wilson for her ideas on creative writing exercises, and also to spiritual friends Gillian Bradshaw, Iris Tute and Chris Stones for our conversations over the years.

I am also grateful for the companionship found in The Thomas Merton Society of Great Britain and Ireland and the St Marylebone Centre for Healing and Counselling.

Thank you to Dan and Gemma for their encouragement and to my husband Peter Ellis, loving companion on the spiritual path, and to whom this book is dedicated.

I would like to thank Virginia Hearn and other staff at Darton, Longman and Todd, for their professional and personal support. Scripture quotations, unless otherwise noted, are from the New Revised Standard Version (Oxford University Press, 1995).

Made in the image of God ... transformed into the likeness of Christ.[1]

The way toward the Homeland becomes more and more obscure. As I look back over the stages which were once more clear, I see that we are all on the right road, and though it be night, it is a saving one. We are very much alone, as regards the crowd which presses in around us. But as regards that 'cloud of witnesses', well that is something altogether different.[2]

CHAPTER ONE

Introducing the four steps

And when you turn to the right or when you turn to the left, your ears shall hear a word behind you, saying, 'This is the way; walk in it.' (Isaiah 30:21)

THERE ARE TIMES IN OUR LIVES when the spiritual journey seems clear, and openings and insights light the way. More usually the path to God can feel hidden – we move in the darkness, and can become very lost. Sometimes we think we have found the way but it turns out to be a dead end. Perhaps the path seems to go nowhere and the journey feels pointless, it's disappointing and sometimes even bleak. At other times we remain stubbornly stuck in the familiar and so we miss opportunities for helpful change. In the quote from Isaiah we are urged to listen, to be really attentive. If we do then we are guided by a word – perhaps even by the Word, Jesus Christ.

We can be attentive to the words that we hear outside us, and, so, we can be guided by the experiences of others. We can also be attentive to the words that we hear inside us, our reflections on our personal experiences. Our developing relationship with God affects us in our inner world and outside in the world. Spiritual teachers from different traditions agree that for each of us there is a specific journey to take and that this is our path to God. Rumi the Sufi mystic writes:

> Heart, you are lost: but there's a path
> From the lover to love, hidden
> But visible. Worlds blaze round you.
> Don't shrink; the path's hidden, but yours.[1]

Abbé de Tourville tells us of the infinite love and compassion God feels towards each of us: 'an intimacy which surpasses all your dreams. Give yourself up with joy to a loving confidence in God and have courage to believe firmly that God's action towards you is a masterpiece of partiality and love.'[2]

In other words, we're all on a path, but it's an individual path. How then can we measure where we are? If it is an individual journey then we are not in competition with each other. Yet we need to understand the obstacles that can hold us up, and the times and places where we may falter and indeed lose courage altogether. It is here then that we need a structure, a framework that we can use as a reference point. We also need some inspiration to help us develop and respond to what life brings us. Often we welcome reading about and making connections to other people's experiences; and finally we need to understand what is happening to us, and how or even why it is or is not happening. This book then offers these four aspects – structure, inspiration, connections with others' experiences, and reflecting on our own spirituality – as a contribution to an understanding of our personal journey to God and the process of being changed.

The four steps of love

The four steps of love described in this book are about being changed. Our spiritual journeying is an experience of continuous conversion. 'To have a conversion experience is nothing much. The real thing is to be able to keep on taking it seriously, to retain a sense of its plausibility.'[3] In other words, the event that sets us out on our spiritual path is in itself either something or nothing – what matters more is the idea of continuous conversion, an ongoing process of inner transformation. This is the path of radical reorientation and of being changed.

Christian conversion, also known as *metanoia,* is about a change of heart, and, as I shall look at in detail in the book, it is about a change of consciousness. This is because it involves a change in the basic values in a person's life, which means a change in direction. If we open ourselves up to God then over time we are changed intellectually, emotionally and morally, as well as spiritually. Once again these changes may only become apparent much later on. At other times we realise the difference in the way we are thinking and responding to a situation. We understand that the difference is one of depth and degree. The previous limits of our personal horizons have been extended. In other words, our deepening love of God enables us to move beyond previous limitations. In this sense our very being changes.

CHAPTER TWO

✢

The idea of continuous conversion

I N THIS CHAPTER the different aspects that provide the framework for the book are described: structure; inspiration; connections and understanding through the experiences of others; and space for reflecting on our own spirituality. The meaning of metanoia – the change of consciousness that we will experience – is explored. After all, we need to know what can happen to us when we begin to open ourselves to God's grace. We also need to acknowledge that, although we may think we want to be closer to God's love through the process of continuous conversion, sometimes another more reluctant part of us will find this difficult, and this too is discussed.

The four steps – the structure

The central structure and reference point used in this book for helping us on our spiritual path is provided by the idea of the four steps of love that St Bernard of Clairvaux described in the twelfth century. The four steps of love are:

> We love ourselves for ourselves.
> We love God for what he gives us.
> We love God for himself.
> We love ourselves for God's sake.

The steps of love were written by St Bernard of Clairvaux as part of what he described as a ladder taking us closer to God; they were used as a method of marking our deepening love and our developing relationship with God. He described each stage in some detail, and they are about the spiritual process of being changed and the long and gradual move to authentic freedom.[1]

In his work *On Loving God*, St Bernard describes the step-by-step progression of the development of love which reaches a state of perfection in the soul that can only be realised in the life to come. He describes the development of love as a mountain to be climbed. However, as with all mountain-climbing the route is rarely straight up the mountain. Indeed it would be naive to think of this as a linear path, for, clearly, there are times when we lose our footing and return to the first step. Perhaps it is more like a spiral path where we visit and revisit old familiar aspects, until we are really ready to move on. More likely, it is a series of frames of mind that we become aware of only to lose. The glimpses that we have are sometimes integrated into our consciousness, and then we realise that we are different. The danger may be that in too much self-consciousness – 'Oh, here I am at step 2' – we defeat the purpose of the recognition. This model is rather to be used as a rough marker in unfamiliar territory. There are problems with the very idea of progression up a ladder; perhaps rather we can think of deepening our sense of the vertical dimension, and our move away from what at times can appear to be only surface.

In this book we explore what the steps of love really mean. We also try to understand their implications for us in the context of the twenty-first century. Can a Cistercian monk who lived between 1090 and 1153 really speak to us in this post-Christian, fragmented and secular age? Well in one sense the steps are offering us a structure for our journey both out of time and space, to what is eternal and timeless. It is also the spiritual journey of each of our lives, and the physical and emotional environment we live in which is within time and space.

One of the ideas that St Bernard implies in the four steps of love is the idea that conversion is an ongoing and deepening process. It is also a process in which God increasingly takes the initiative. As we start to explore the four steps of love we see that it is partly about the experience of grace. If we can hold to the idea that 'God's action towards us is a masterpiece of partiality and love',[2] then we can begin to grasp the immensity of the changes that can happen to us in a life of faith. We are gradually drawn towards God, and the realisation of the centre of a different sort of reality than that which we thought we knew.

The four questions – the inspiration

If St Bernard's four steps of love give us the structure then the Bible is the source of inspiration as we take our steps on this journey. It's not only the stories and accounts of others' experiences in the Bible that can inspire us, but also the questions that are asked of us. One of the ways in which we open ourselves to change and development is by asking questions. If we ask a question, whether of ourselves or somebody else, we open ourselves to the possibility of something new. We may hear something different from what we expected. Sometimes we are encouraged to make changes when we try to give answers to questions. When we ask, it implies that we are seeking an answer, and the question and answer both contain our desire to find something out and the values connected to that search.

Paul Tillich, the theologian and philosopher, was struck as a child by the question, 'Why is there something rather than nothing?'[3] As a child, the root of the questioning may

6

have lain in his own near-death experiences as a baby, and the untimely death of his mother when he was seventeen, and this is the question he returned to again and again as an adult. For Paul Tillich, being human means that we can make judgements and understand that something is not real or does not occur because we are aware of the distinction between being and non-being. In other words, we can ask why there is something instead of nothing. In our very ability to ask questions about our life, and its meaning, we are asking theological questions. Paul Tillich thought that with the capacity to raise such theological questions we also are ultimately concerned about the answers. In other words, we come to see ourselves in the light of the answers we are given, or give to ourselves. Science, philosophy and psychology only give us an incomplete answer because they exclude the concern about our very existence. We search for what the answers mean for us. For Paul Tillich, the content of Christian revelation genuinely answers the question that people ask *qua* human beings. In his experience and thinking, Christian belief answers the ultimate concern which underlies all the religious and cultural questioning of the race, in the past, present and future.[4] In that sense, Christian belief is for him the universal answer to the questions about the meaning of life.

Sometimes the universal questioning becomes particular. 'What is it that I want? What is the experience of God in my own life?' Joel Giallanza warns that questions about one's own spiritual journey should not be random or accidental, but rather that they should facilitate choices which have to be made, 'should be a guide along the road, should offer the support and the challenge necessary to continue faithfully even when the road is dark'.[5] He wonders where these questions are to be found and suggests the Bible, and in particular the questions asked by Jesus Christ. The questions Jesus asks in the gospel accounts are questions that are also intended for us – here and now. They are questions about our individual spiritual journey, and they are also universal questions.

In both Testaments of the Bible it's often the case that a moment of revelation, a sudden insight and new aware-ness, is marked by a question. All sorts of people ask ques-tions in the Bible and listen to the answers. If we question, we are asking for something; whether we change depends on what we do with the answer. Responding depends on our receptivity. If we are questioned we may start to step outside of our ordinary thinking, and that may lead to a moment of realisation and a moment of inspiration. Through this book, Jesus Christ asks each of us four ques-tions – questions from the gospels that ask us to listen and to be attentive. We don't always need to come up with an answer but they offer us a space for individual reflection, and can help us on the journey of becoming the likeness of Christ.

Understanding and being affected through connecting with the experiences of others

It can feel lonely sometimes on the spiritual path – these are not the easiest experiences to share, and usually there are only a few people available or appropriate to talk about them with. However, Thomas Merton says that we are not alone because we are surrounded by the cloud of witnesses, and some of these have written down their experiences for us. In their accounts we get the personal sense of conversion and their ongoing struggles on the path. Reading about their lives gives us both deep insights into their relationship with God, and some guidance for ourselves. It is really through other narratives that we can get an understanding of the impact of the mysteries of faith and our spiritual journey. In this book the words of others are used to help us understand what may be happening to each of us.

It often seems that those who most inspire us are those with whom we can make a connection. If we look at their lives we see in turn those who inspired them, and those with whom they made a connection. The same process takes us back on a continuous trail. Friedrich von Hügel attributed all he knew to Huvelin, and quotes Lucretius that, 'One torch lights another torch.' We learn, von Hügel writes, as 'one penitent soul awakens to the desire to teach other souls ... it is best to learn from others; it gives a touch of creatureliness'. This is not to say that we expect to have the same experiences: 'Your ultimate light is your own; but in the meantime you have got to learn.'[6]

It seems that when we enter truly into the mystery of another person, we are inevitably encouraged to look more deeply at our self. As we deepen our spiritual searching so we are taken into the divine mystery. One example is Henri Nouwen, who considered the work of Vincent van Gogh to have been theologically significant and personally meaningful in his own life. He wrote of the connections between his own and the painter's struggles. He wrote that Vincent van Gogh painted, 'what I had not before dared to look at; he questioned what I had not before dared to speak about; and he entered into the spaces of my heart that I had not dared to come close to'. Henri Nouwen understood that this connection led him to confront his own fears and gave him the courage to deepen his search for a loving God.[7]

These are spiritual threads that link us to one another beyond chronological time. In this book I look at the experiences of those who have been searching for a loving God in their own lives. Most of those to whom I turn are now part of the heavenly community, but still can inspire and lead us on the path of the four steps of love. As noted already, the earthly inspiration that lies behind the book is the work of St Bernard, 'a spiritual master, a theologian of the search for God',[8] who translated his spiritual experiences into a form that can still hold meaning for us. He understood that all we need is to set free the image of God which is within each of us. With that the realisation comes that we need something, someone beyond our self. It is our innate longing that sets us on the path, and grace that guides us and prompts us to discover spiritual freedom through the four steps of love.

In each generation the spirit is revived and renewed. One hymn-writer expressed it as the breath of life that sweeps through us: 'O Breath of Love, come breathe within us, renewing thought and will and heart; come, love of Christ, afresh to win us, and fit your Church to meet this hour.'[9]

Reflecting on our own spiritual journey

The four questions that Jesus asks us in the gospels are central to the Christian faith and the personal spiritual journey and can be linked directly to St Bernard's four steps of love. Each step of love seems to suggest a question and each question seems to lead us further into the step. The answers given by those who were asked in the biblical narrative and others who have walked on the same journey that we are on can serve as signposts for our own responses. Of course we need to find ourselves in a position where we are asked and ask these questions, and where we can have time and space to reflect on our answers. The book is divided into sections that correspond to the four steps and four questions, and throughout are quoted the experiences of others. At the end of the chapters, linked to each step and question, are some practical ideas – exercises, suggestions, thoughts and prayers. These can offer personal discovery time and may be ways to enter further into the ideas developed in the book.

Metanoia – a change in consciousness

One way of thinking about the spiritual change that happens through the four steps of love – the questions we are asked, and understanding both through the experiences of others and our own reflections – is referring to it as a change of heart, and we might talk about a change of mind. It is all part of our deepening relationship with God. Taken together it adds up to a change in consciousness. The change of consciousness that happens through the four steps of love and the questions that Jesus Christ asks us to think about takes place in us intellectually, emotionally and morally, and may also affect us physically. Our mind, our feelings, our attitude to our body, and our very conscience are altered through the love of God. It may be that there are also different emphases for each of us. One route for conversion and the ladder to God may be predominantly through feelings and experiences; another comes through the mind and our intellect; and the third through moral concerns and a change in our moral conscience. For all of us there will be a profound change in all aspects of our lives as we gradually change the centre of our being from self to God.

St Bernard's model of the ladder and the four steps of love that lead us to God imply changes in the gradations of our consciousness. In the Indian yogic tradition Sri Aurobindo, in his *Letters on Yoga*, writes about spiritual transformation as 'something dynamic ... It means a bringing down of the Divine Consciousness, static and dynamic, into all these parts (mind, heart, life and body) and the entire replacement of the present consciousness by that.'[10]

What does a change of consciousness really mean? It is about a continuous deepening of our spiritual awareness. One useful way of thinking about this process is to imagine our spiritual consciousness as made up of different layers. Some aspects are hidden, and are then uncovered, they are initially unconscious and then brought into consciousness. Others are on the threshold of our awareness, and may need just a nudge or a glimpse to emerge so that we become aware of them and the implications of our experiences. We often become aware of things changing through glimpses, sudden insights, dreams, intimations, consolations and sudden moments of intense joy. The deeper changes we may not see until we have worked through them. As we travel along the four steps of love so there is an increase in spiritual awareness that in time suffuses our entire state of consciousness. What was previously part of our spiritual unconscious is now part of our growing awareness. In this process of continuous conversion, God becomes integrated into our conscious life. We are alive and realise that our life is within God – we are changing within God and through God.

In the Old Testament, especially in the psalms, we read about the movement from disorientation to orientation. The psalmists often begin in misery, but experience a turn and transformation. For example, in Psalm 13 the first verse begins, 'How long, O LORD? Will you forget me for ever?' and ends with verse 6, 'I will sing to the LORD, because he has dealt bountifully with me.' This 'structure of transformation permeates the entire Old Testament'.[11] In both Testaments of the Bible there is an aspect of mutuality in relationship between God and those who turn to him: 'Return to me, and I will return to you' (Malachi 3:7b). For the Christian, conversion involves entering into a special, personal relationship with God through Christ: 'a new relationship with Christ … is the definition of Christian conversion.'[12] Walter Conn writes about Christian conversion as a process of falling in love: 'one's being must become a being-in-love.' He quotes Bernard Lonergan who explicitly understands such religious conversion as the proper fulfilment of one's capacity for self-transcendence. It is not only a turning to God, but rather a radical reorientation so that God (not just religious ideas, aims and interests) becomes the centre and principal reality of that life.[13] Conversion is ultimately not to a particular denomination but to Christ and into his likeness.

Realising the reluctance to change

This process and talk of being affected, becoming changed and radically reorientated can disturb us, and part of getting stuck on the spiritual journey may be when we resist anything different. We dig in our heels, and refuse to hear and be attentive to what is happening around and inside us. Perhaps we feel very defensive, or rubbish what we are experiencing. Perhaps we start to think it all a bit irrational, or it does not fit with our own ideas and expectations. Why would we resist in this way? Sometimes it can be frightening to feel that we are becoming different or thinking differently. After all it's part of human nature to prefer the familiar and the predictable, and we are reluctant to lose our sense of control – or rather the illusion that everything is under our control. Everything that happens to us affects us, but sometimes we are able to 'have the experience', in other words we think we are in charge. Often in the life of faith it's more as if 'the experience is having us'. Sometimes even if we reject the experiences they still break through, despite our best efforts to deny them. One of the most difficult things about developing spiritually is leaving behind whatever we have outgrown. If we grow, then we lose something of how we have been. Changing puts a new demand on us. Conversion as an ongoing process leads us to a change of consciousness and a change of heart. It is also about a difference in our relationship with God and we may have mixed feelings about this too.

So acknowledging our longings and our reluctance we begin our exploration of the four steps of love, and we also begin to think about the four questions that Jesus asks us in this book. In the next two chapters we look at the first step and the first question. This is followed by some ideas for personal reflection. We also look at the experiences of those who are searching, and the universal and deeply familiar longings to find a radically loving God. The process of continuous conversion, the spiritual journey on the four steps of love, is a path of inner transformation – it is about becoming changed during our life. We are born in the image of God, and, as we live, our destiny is to be changed into the likeness of Christ.

CHAPTER THREE

The first step of love:
'We love ourselves for ourselves'

THE FIRST STEP OF LOVE on St Bernard's ladder to God is that we love ourselves for our own sake. When St Bernard writes about this first step he sees it as inevitable that we put our physical needs and natural desires first. We need to survive physically, and so we do all we can to ensure that. He describes this as 'carnal' love. In this first step of love we are only aware of ourselves. Love is part of our natural make-up and to begin with it is self-orientated, so we look after ourselves. St Bernard understood that as part of this first step of love we can move out of self-preoccupation and extend this same love towards others. He warns against keeping things for ourselves, and urges us to share with our neighbour. 'Thus carnal love becomes social when it is extended to others.'[1] I think here he is talking about sharing food, shelter and warmth. If we begin to share the things we need for our physical well-being with others then this opens us to God. This might begin in our family and among our friends. In other words, when we take our self-centred love and reach out to others this action brings God into our lives. This may be particularly true if in our efforts to give to others we start to appreciate

15

our own loss – that we then have less or even not enough – and so we turn to God for help.

Self-preoccupation

Clearly loving ourselves is a good thing – indeed in the commandment Jesus reminds us, 'You shall love your neighbour as yourself' (Matthew 22:39) – but in contemporary terms the first step of love may be more about a distorted form of self-love that does not really involve anyone else at all. It is not just about meeting our physical needs, but also about the primacy of our psychological needs above anyone else – it's about 'me, me, and just me'! In other words it's not genuine self-love, but rather a preoccupation with our self. We sometimes call it narcissism, and after all this is a narcissistic age – it's all about looking out for number one, finding pleasure in how we are and how we appear. Everything that happens to us is filtered through the narrow lens of what it does for us, for our personal or professional development, and everyone we meet is assessed in terms of what they can do for us. Perhaps in this frame of mind we feel self-important, we relish our uniqueness. We may like to be the centre of things, and react badly to being criticised or defeated by someone in a discussion or in a game. In our relationships we expect things from others and don't, or perhaps we can't, reciprocate. Perhaps we like to control how others react and behave, and we certainly aren't able to really imagine what it must be like for them. Alternatively the form that our self-love takes can be one of negativity and hatred – no less preoccupying. We are taken up with our own misery, and can find meaning in hurting and hating ourselves and through that others. One time we love our self, another time we hate our self, but the focus of our energy is firmly focused on us.

None of it sounds very attractive, and yet it's certainly a stage we all directly experience – perhaps especially when we are adolescent. Unfortunately it's also a state of mind that we often retreat to as adults – usually when we are feeling under attack or stressed. We can feel narcissistically vulnerable and wounded – our sense of who we are is threatened, and so we react and protect ourselves. And of course there are many reasons to get stuck at this first step. Some of the reasons will belong in the past, and yet still cast a long shadow affecting our present and future. We can also get stuck on different levels. We can get stuck at the surface level of superficial materialism, or we can get stuck in a place of deep and stagnant self-reflection, dissecting our every action and thought.

In his autobiography, Thomas Merton captures the superficial attraction of loving ourselves for ourselves. As a student he describes a thoroughly contemporary and cosmopolitan life made up of films, jazz, nightclubs, drinking, relationships with women and dabbling in politics – a series of fragmented and ultimately unsatisfactory experiences. He is looking for a chance to savour the world and all that is on offer, and four years after leaving school he writes that he had at last 'become a true child of the modern world completely tangled up in petty and useless concerns with myself, and almost incapable of even considering or understanding anything that was really important to my own true interests'. In savouring the pleasures he notes the paradox: 'In filling myself, I had emptied myself. In grasping things, I had lost everything. In devouring pleasures and joys, I had found distress and anguish and fear.'[2]

Augustine of Hippo, writing of the years before his conversion, describes our attraction to things that cannot last and to the material. After an adventurous youth, attracted to a 'set of sensualists', he was drawn to become a serious thinker and scholar, but sees later that still, 'my thoughts ranged only among material forms'.[3]

Self-preoccupation and God

It is quite possible to be very caught up in oneself, and also believe in God. It's just that if we are not really open to others, let alone to God, then our conception of God will be extremely limited. In fact the god that we allow in our lives will be predetermined by our own needs. We may construct a good or bad god who exists only to fulfil our own needs, or to reflect our psychic make-up. This god can be a punishing, hateful tormentor, or a cold, indifferent figure. It can be a god who agrees with everything we do, who condones our selfish actions, or a god who only loves us if we are falsely compliant and submissive. It can be an out-there god who has no impact on us and whom we only bring out on special occasions or when we want to be seen as religious. There is an infinite variety, but all these constructions are fundamentally narcissistic, and only a projection of our own state of mind. There is then no need for any spiritual growth or conversion because nothing real is actually happening, and nothing real is going to happen.

If we become stuck here then we are only returning the favour that God created us in his image by in turn fashioning a god in our image again and again. This is then not a God that is more than our self, but a god that is a projection of a part of our self. This is the god whom we use to bolster our political beliefs or our particular actions. It is an idol that reflects back part of us.

The move from self-preoccupation to self-love

Whatever the form it takes and whether we have a religious life or not, self-preoccupation is not a happy state of mind, and so most of us, if we can, reach out to connect with others, not just for what we can get from them, but with a more genuine motive of sharing and relating. We may also begin to question who we are and why we are the way we are, and so as we begin to look for meaning in our life through relating to others, we step out of the tight circle of our imprisoned self.

To open ourselves to others means that we have to accept who we are and how we are. We have to stop being so concerned about our life, and start being concerned about someone else's. This needs some self-awareness about how we behave and the effect we have on others – both good and bad. It means letting go of some fantasised idealised self and our own uniqueness. It also means relinquishing our self-consciousness about having material things or spiritual experiences that make us feel better or special, or, conversely, our obsessing about how awful we are and how we deserve all that happens to us, including the contempt of others. It means a more realistic love and acceptance of who we are. With this self-awareness we can open ourselves in a genuine way to others and so we stop being totally preoccupied with what is happening to us, and begin to care about what is happening to the other person or to people.

Beginning to search on the spiritual path

When we reach out to relationships with others and through that towards God, I think we are looking for something more than ourselves. Moving away from the first step of love probably begins when we realise that things are not right. Our life, including the god whom we have constructed, is ultimately unsatisfactory. Perhaps we are not happy, or feel dissatisfied by the way we live, or we may wonder about the meaning of life and our place in the world. We may be in a place of deep suffering, and so we become desperate, questioning and wondering about our lives. One way or another there is an opening in the fortress we have constructed around us, and so we start our searching. Another way of thinking about this would be that we begin to be open to being found. We begin to open ourselves to the possibility of God's love and grace.

Before we are able to receive God's love and grace we need some inner space. In order to see the light we need to remove, or have removed, some of the obstacles and clutter that preoccupy us and our own mediocrity. This labyrinth of our own self-love that eventually leads nowhere has also obscured the path of God's love. As we turn towards that path and release some space, the groundwork of conversion begins to take place. Both our inner and outer horizons begin to shift. Almost inevitably it will be a process where some of our most rigid defences, rationalisations and self-orientated thinking become dismantled. The Muslim mystic Rumi likens the self-preoccupied state of mind to a prison.

> Why when God's world is so big,
> did you fall asleep in a prison
> of all places?[4]

Moving forward from the first step of love and opening ourselves to others and to God is the groundwork of conversion and implies a loosening of those prison bars. It also involves the recognition of our resistance to any serious change. It suggests a growing awareness that may be emerging in our spiritual consciousness. In other words we are on the threshold of something new, although again we are usually unaware of what is happening to us. Perhaps one crucial defence that needs to be relinquished is the illusion that we are in control. This may be especially difficult if we have spent years building up our sense of ourselves and now believe that we can make choices for our own spiritual well-being. Accepting that our grip on life is an illusion is an insight that allows something more than ourselves to affect us. Sometimes the groundwork of conversion, and the opening of horizons, takes place through the inspiration of another person who shows us that there may be another perspective to the way we are thinking. Sometimes we can be especially open to change when our life is difficult or we are faced with some disaster or suffering and loss. If we are shaken in the illusion of our control we then have space for God's action and can make a genuine move in our spiritual journeying.

Becoming hungry

Once we begin to search we may start to realise that we are hungry for something different. It's not just the realisation that our hamster-wheel existence isn't enough, but the questioning, 'Is this it? Is this all my life is?', articulates our hunger for God, though we may not recognise the concept of God. When we are first born our mouths know about longing, and quickly realise that good things come from outside us, they are not our possession. Our first experience as babies is that reality is 'not made up of "thought" and "matter" as we have been taught'. Rather reality is, 'made up of "hunger" and of an "obscure object of desire", which will satisfy it'. The mouth 'sucks the void, confident that it exists'.[5] In the same way there is within us all a hunger for God, and if we open our self to him we can be fed and filled. This is the spiritual dimension present in each of us.

As one theologian notes, we are what we eat and 'the whole world is presented as one all-embracing banquet table'. This is an image that permeates the Bible and remains the central image of life. It is 'the image of life at its creation and also at its end and fulfilment: "that you eat and drink at my table in my kingdom"'.[6] The psalmist urges us: 'O taste and see that the LORD is good' (Psalm 34:8). Once we realise how hungry we are, we can begin to take God inside us, and the forgotten and hidden experience of God starts to satisfy us. In the next chapter Jesus Christ asks us in his first question to move from the prison of self-preoccupation to be fed by God's love.

CHAPTER FOUR

The first question:
'What are you looking for?'

J ESUS' FIRST QUESTION IS TO two future disciples who
are searching. He turns and see them approaching and
asks, 'What are you looking for?' (John 1:38). Often as we
step outside of our own immediate desires we don't know
what it is we are looking for. We are looking, like Paul
Tillich, for something instead of nothing. Perhaps we are
still looking for something that will fulfil us, perhaps at a
deeper level we are looking for a more real part of ourselves. Perhaps we are looking for something that is hidden
deep in our spiritual unconscious. Perhaps we are looking
for something that is already within us. In this chapter we
explore what the question might be about and what might
be meant by the idea of the spiritual unconscious. Thinking
about the answer to this question is the groundwork of our
present conversion towards God. We are moving towards
St Bernard's second step of love.

Looking for the unthought known

Augustine believes that we are born with a longing for connection with God. He writes that 'Our hearts are restless',

and this restlessness remains until we find union with God: 'Lord, you have made us for yourself, and our hearts are restless till they rest in you.' In his own spiritual journey he describes his increasing despair as he walked 'on a treacherous path, in darkness'. He was in the dark because he was, 'looking for God outside myself and I did not find the God of my own heart'. Augustine asks what it means to be born in the likeness of God. In his questioning he was searching for certainty and answers.[1]

We are born with this 'unthought known',[2] a longing to make a connection with God, a longing hidden deep within our very being, which impels us to search. In other words, we look for something we are already familiar with but that we cannot yet recognise. As we open ourselves to God, the unthought known can begin to become the thought known. Our earliest encounters with God are 'unthought' in the sense that they are experiences, and not reasoned logic. Some people have described this as a form of infant spirituality to which we all have access as babies and small children. William Wordsworth famously described the baby as 'trailing clouds of glory'; in other words, he thought that we brought the sense of, and openness to, heaven with us as we were born. As we grow older we are gradually claimed by the realities of life. The 'bars of the prison house begin to close', and we lose contact with what we have once known.[3]

This suggests that we already know in a pre-verbal form the sense or feel of what much later we are looking for spiritually. This is the heightened wonder, amazement and awe that we can experience when we really look and see what it is we are looking at. It seems a wonder more accessible when we are small children, and can be understood as spirituality without words. Such visions have been described as contact with 'that territory where the unknown lives',[4] and also as 'something that shines into the childhood of all and in which no one has yet been: home-land'.[5] The psalmist speaks of this in Psalm 8:2 (NIV): 'From the lips of children and infants you have ordained praise.'

Such encounters with oneness and the connection with creation gradually become trivialised, reduced or denied once they are framed in language; they also eventually become repressed and buried. Most of us forget our initial excitement with nature, and our sense of awe and wonder with the numinous and the supernatural. The state of high amazement is jaded, and all is accepted as commonplace and adjusted to as we grow into the world. The amazing sight of thousands of leaves filled with light and sound becomes just another tree – and once you've seen one you've seen them all.

The idea of the spiritual unconscious

Such infant and childhood experiences of the numinous quality of creation sink into our unconscious along with the dissociated feelings from personally painful events and relationships. There is then a mixture of wonder and fear that forms the bedrock of what is our spiritual unconscious. The 'unthought known' is buried in our spiritual uncon-scious, and every so often we catch a glimpse or hear an echo that propels us to keep looking. Perhaps there are odd moments when once again we are filled with the wonder of the created world. Our earliest searching for God may later seem to have been irrational and largely intuitive, but it is a felt experience that is now repressed, and yet still present, buried in our psyche – ready to re-emerge. We feel the sub-jective experience before any recognition, and in time reconciliation with God takes place. We are seeking for something that is not apparently present but that already exists within us. As shown in the old Christian proverb:

'You would not search for Me if you had not first known Me', which suggests that somewhere we do know what we are looking for, but for all sorts of reasons it is just not accessible in our consciousness. In his memoirs Mircea Eliade comments on a note that he made after reading some of the Upanishads: 'God (= The Spirit) is buried in us as in a cave; he isn't dead, but only hidden somewhere in there.'[6]

Nicolas Berdyaev wrote about his dim apprehension, even as a child, 'of religious life as a realm of inward spiritual revelation, which by being exteriorised loses its authentic character'.[7] Our earliest spiritual encounters are inevitably wordless – they happen to all of us before we can speak. We then struggle to mentally represent through language and known concepts these different experiences and sensations. Our spiritual infancy, perhaps we could call it infant mysticism, is then an unarticulated or unconscious religious experience, almost a sort of pantheism characterised by wonder and awe.

So – 'What are you looking for?'

This question that Jesus asks us here and now offers us a chance for spiritual awakening. As we reflect on what our answer might be we are open to all possibilities. In other words, we are in a place of becoming, for going beyond ourselves, and so we carry the potential for conversion and moving to the second step of love. As we start to conceptualise and frame our experiences verbally, what was unknown becomes thought and even thoughtful. However, it may also be that at that point of answering the question and naming and describing the experience, we limit and deny, and in the reduction lose some part of it.

The way that we start to answer this question, 'What are you looking for?', will be influenced by our particular attraction towards the intellectual, the emotional and the moral. It is at this point that the grace of God helps us in our search. In this way, as we move forward on the four steps of love, God acts as a transformational process who, through continuous action within us, alters our very being – mind, heart and soul. Continuous conversion becomes transformational action. God transforms our very being by bringing our spiritual needs, our unthought known, into our conscious awareness. Part of the transforming process is to enable us to grow closer to Jesus Christ through a relationship in which we can articulate, recognise and elaborate our own true self. As Friedrich von Hügel wrote: 'Christianity is a thing of the heart … No other knowledge counts but that that feeds and strengthens the mind and soul.' Gwendolen Greene, in her introduction to the letters her uncle Friedrich von Hügel wrote to her, remembers his advice to her as she began her search:

> Live all you can – as complete and full a life as you can find – do as much as you can for others. Read, work, enjoy – love and help as many souls – do all this. Yes – but remember: be alone, be remote, be away from the world, be desolate. Then you will be near God.[8]

Thomas Merton uses the image of a crystal – a potentially lucid crystal left in darkness: 'It is perfect in its own nature, but it lacks something that it can only receive from outside and above itself.'[9] When a ray of light strikes the crystal, the crystal becomes transformed into light, and its very nature is altered. The ray of light can be filtered through our intellect, our feelings or our moral sense. In a way, all are interconnected, but usually one aspect will predominate in us.

The beginnings of intellectual conversion

Some spiritual writers document intellectual insight as their answer to this question and the central part of the groundwork of their conversion. One example is that of Raissa and Jacques Maritain. In her autobiography Raissa Maritain writes that she was a questioning student, searching and hungry for meaning in life. Her answer to the question 'What are you looking for?' would have been that she was looking for truth. Both she and Jacques initially searched for this through academic study:

> I was truly seeking only that which I needed to justify existence, that which should seem to me, myself, necessary in order that human life be not a thing absurd and cruel. I needed the joy of understanding, the light of certitude, a rule of life based on faultless truth.

Jacques Maritain shared Raissa's concern for the search for truth. Together they vowed to commit suicide if they failed in their search for truth and meaning:

> If we must give up the hope of finding any meaning whatever for the word truth, for the distinction of good from evil, of just from unjust, it is no longer possible to live humanely ... I wanted no part in such a comedy. I would have accepted a sad life, but not one that was absurd.[10]

'It was then that God's pity caused us to find Henri Bergson.' Raissa and Jacques, began to attend the lectures of Henri Bergson in the winter of 1901, following the recommendation of a friend. His acceptance of intuition, and above all his confidence in the existence of an unchanging order accessible to human understanding, allowed Raissa Maritain to begin to believe that attainment of 'the Absolute' was a possibility. Henri Bergson's lectures allowed her the freedom to think about the inward activity of the mind, and, 'the entirely qualitative depths of consciousnesses'. The benefits were 'the horizons he opened to us – away from the empty and colourless world of universal mechanism and toward the universe of qualities, toward spiritual certainty, toward personal liberty'.[11] In this way for them the answer to Jesus' question took place through intellectual inspiration.

Sometimes the light comes and strikes us through something we read, and this can have both an intellectual and emotional impact. For Thomas Merton, the groundwork of his conversion and the opening of horizons he partly traces back to the impact of a book called *The Spirit of Medieval Philosophy* by Etienne Gilson. The response to the question 'What are you looking for?' is, at this stage of his life, to do with academic success, and the book he thinks will be useful for his French medieval literature course. He does not see until on the bus on the way home that this is a Catholic book. Tempted to throw the book out of the window, full of disgust at the apparent deception – he should have been warned it was a Catholic book – he nevertheless reads some of it, and one idea strikes him. This is the concept of *aseitas* – which offers an entirely new concept of God. The meaning is that God exists by reason of himself, God is Being Itself. Years later at the monastery Thomas Merton sees the pencil note he made on reading this concept, 'Aseity of God, God is being per se'. He also marked other sections, including the idea that God transcends all our conceptions – especially those that are impossible. Here, for Thomas Merton, is the appreciation that he is no longer in control of whether God exists. God exists whatever he, Thomas Merton, believes and in a way that he can barely approach, let alone understand.

> What a relief for me, now, to discover not only that no idea of ours, let alone any image, could adequately represent God, but also that we should not allow ourselves to be satisfied with any such knowledge of Him.[12]

The effect of this book was to give Thomas Merton an intellectual respect for Catholic philosophy and faith. It also shifted him emotionally, in that he began to see that faith had a clear meaning, and a reason to be considered. Reading the book began to change his response to the question, 'What are you looking for?' There were now different possibilities that contributed to the groundwork of his conversion.

The beginnings of emotional conversion

Our world is interpreted through our emotions as well as intellectually and morally. Often our emotions colour the intellectual and moral choices that we make. Part of what we can understand about an emotional conversion involves our passionate feelings towards God. The groundwork of conversion can take place through loving someone else, a partner, a friend, a child, an animal – all expressions of true love open us to God.

Etty Hillesum, writing during the Second World War, experienced the groundwork of conversion through such emotional changes. We can be hugely influenced by those whom we meet, and Etty Hillesum describes the opening of psychological horizons that took place in the company of Julius Spier, the founder of 'psychochirology', who had been trained in analysis by Carl Jung in Zurich. Etty Hillesum finds in him the answer to her 'spiritual constipation'. Using breathing exercises, the unorthodox practice of physically wrestling with him, as well as talking to him about her depression, Etty Hillesum feels herself changing. She begins to love him and want to be with him. In such ways the relationship with another can emotionally change us and open us to spiritual conversion.

Suddenly I was living differently, more freely, more

30

flowingly; the costive feeling vanished, a little calm and order came into my life, at first entirely under the influence of his magical personality, but gradually with the assent of my own psyche, of my own awareness.[13]

The beginnings of moral conversion

Moral conversion involves our conscience, not the censorious, critical, negative idea of the superego put forward by Freud, but the ethical, responsible part of us. This is the part of us that is taken up by moral judgements, decisions and choices about human existence. Johannes Jorgensen, a Danish writer who later converted to Catholicism, was troubled by the temporality of existence, and from childhood he was searching for some solution to the 'consciousness that the present existence is unique, that there is no other', a dilemma that 'would not leave me, and kept hold of my heart in a crushing grip'. Instead of God, Johannes Jorgensen looked for a personal system of belief and turned to poets and philosophers, and what he describes as 'all the melancholy, despairing and rebellious literature of the period'. He saw himself as a rebel and an outsider at war with society. In answer to the question 'What are you looking for?' he wrote of wanting something instead of the feeling of everlasting emptiness to which he awoke every morning and which no philosophy could fill.[14]

Sooner or later we are all confronted with questioning the meaning of things beyond the fulfilment of our personal needs. Sometimes the question 'What are you looking for?' leads to other intellectual, emotional and moral questions. What do I think of this strange world? Is it all chance, or is there a hidden purpose to it? Is it possible to believe in a God who is concerned for each of us? Why is there so much suffering? What does evil mean? What happens when I die – is there part of me that survives the death of the physical body? Who am I anyway? Why am I the way I am? Where can I find the truth? Sometimes these questions about morals lead us to God, or to take part in social action and the search for justice in the world.

Our conscience develops through moral conversion; this is a conversion where we become increasingly attuned to moral values and less caught up in the concrete material reality. Our questioning is the universal search for the redeeming answer – the crystallising thoughts on the meaning of life. Constant questioning is unsettling, but it also grounds us in the situations that surround us. Our spiritual questioning cannot end in answers that are certain or unambiguous, but it does lead us towards God.

The hunger, longing and confusion about what we are looking for does lead us to consciously question what we are doing in our life, and it sometimes leads us to try to find an answer. By struggling to reach a place of thought about a deep existential 'knowing' within us we start to build up the groundwork of our conversion, horizons gradually open before us, and we begin to break through the prison of the false self that we have built up around us, and so touch on central aspects of our true self. In the next chapter we spend a little longer on exploring this move from the first step and our answers to the first question and begin to look at the implications of a personal relationship with God. Before that are some practical suggestions that link directly to the first step and the first question.

Practical suggestions linked to the first step of love and the first question

Exercise 1: What is in my life?

- Draw a circle and divide it into four parts.
    One quarter is for work – what you do with your day (paid or not).
    One quarter is for close relationships – family and intimate relationships.
    One quarter is for friendships and interests.
    One quarter is for spirituality and religion.
- Over a week, fill each quarter and see how much time is allotted for each.
- At the end of the week you may see what is missing. Is your circle balanced?

Exercise 2: What really matters to me?

Here is a list of values, qualities and ideas. Circle ten that seem most important to you. If some are missing, then add them. Then see if you can reduce that to five and finally to three – you should arrive at what really matters to you.

Adventure, Beauty, Church, Community, Competence, Creativity, Culture, Democracy, Ecology, Ethical behaviour, Fame, Family, Fast living, Freedom, Friendship, God, Good food, Health, Hobbies, Holidays, Home, Honour, Independence, Influence, Inner harmony, Intellectual status, Jesus, Job security, Joy, Keeping fit, Knowledge, Leadership, Love and affection, Loyalty, Meaningfulness, Openness, Order, Peace, Personal growth, Politics, Power, Privacy, Public service, Purity, Quality of relations, Quality of what I do, Recognition, Relationships, Religion, Responsibility, Security, Self-esteem, Serenity, Shopping, Spirituality, Status, Travel, Truth, Wealth, Wisdom; Any others.

Then there are two questions to be answered:

- What am I living for?
- What is keeping me from living fully for the thing I want to live for?

Suggestions

Learning to really listen

The next time you meet a friend or an acquaintance who wants to talk and you have the time, practise learning to really listen to another person.

Try to keep regular eye contact (though not continuous staring) and concentrate on giving total and clear attention – keep your own mind free from rehearsing replies or mentally making comparisons with your own situation. Try to focus completely on being receptive to the person who is speaking. It sounds easy but it's often difficult to be really open to the other person – notice how often you want to jump in and make it better or give advice, and how hard it is to stop yourself.

Practise this in relationships and then practise this with God. Set aside some time where you will not be interrupted, and try to be quiet with God for ten minutes and listen intently. If we are intent on listening then we do not think and our mind is clear. We become aware.

Gradually bring your attention in from the external noises outside of where you are to the nearer noises. Then listen to the noise of your breathing and your heartbeat. Listen intently to the silence for God. Beyond the sound of the breath is what is described as the hum of creation.

Developing awareness through relaxation and breathing

These are both practices that can help us to be open to God. They need to be done on a regular basis.

Relaxation: honouring the body

Look at your body – part by part. Is your body a familiar friend, or is it the enemy or something to be ashamed of? Think about the parts you like and think are lovely and the parts you don't like and think are ugly. Bring your body into your conscious awareness and stand as you are in front of God, honouring his creation: 'God created me and sees that I am good.' In God's sight we need not reject, punish or indulge our bodies, but instead understand our needs and take them seriously. Learn to relax by lying down and bringing a loving awareness to each part of the body.

Breathing: honouring the spirit

Sit upright with your back straight; close your eyes and breathe through your nose. Count each breath as you breathe out. Breathe in – out (one), breathe in – out (two), until you reach ten, then return to one.

This is an exercise to practise until you can concentrate on the breath for 15 minutes. You can also learn to control the breath by alternate nostril breathing (closing in turn each nostril – the aim is to practise concentration and awareness). Later the practice can be extended to note the breath as it moves deeper into our chest and abdomen and out again. In other words we envisage the spirit of God moving through us and awakening us in love.

Prayers

1. Lord, let me be a learner in your school of prayer.[15]
2. Let your mercy, O Lord, be upon us, and the brightness of

your Spirit lighten the deepest parts of our being. Kindle our cold hearts and light up our dark minds that we may be open to your loving presence, through Jesus Christ, Amen.

3. Friedrich von Hügel recommended the following prayer by St Ignatius to his niece when she began her spiritual quest. He suggested that if it made sense to her she should begin each day with it:

> Receive, O Lord, my entire liberty – my understanding, my memory, my will. From Thee have I received all things – to Thee do I return all things. Give me but Thy Grace and Thy Love. I ask not anything else of Thee.[16]

Thought

Now, in the light of that last prayer, have a think about the implications of this joke story. Some jokes, like this one, contain an element of truth:

> This man was driving in his car on a mountainous road. Unfortunately he missed a crucial turn and the car went plunging into the ravine below. He just managed to grab onto a small tree that was sticking out of the side of the mountain. He's hanging there with one hand and shouting out, 'Help! Help!' All he gets back is his own echo: 'Help! Help!' 'Is anybody there to help me?' 'Is anybody there to help me?' So, finally he says, 'God, are you there? Can you help me?' God answers him and says, 'Yes, I'm here and I can help you.' He says, 'Well hurry, my arm is giving out.' So God says to him, 'Do you believe in me?' and he says, 'Yes, I believe in you.' So God says, 'Well, if you believe in me, let go of the tree.' There's a long pause, then the man says, 'Can anyone else help me?'[17]

Only after thinking about this joke is it wise to really mean the prayer that Friedrich von Hügel recommended. After all, do we really want to trust this presence in our lives, can we let go into what is so unknown, or can we afford not to?

CHAPTER FIVE

From the first step of love
to the second

A S WE SET OUT on our spiritual journey, so the question
'What are you looking for?' stays with us and keeps
our mind open to the idea of God, and from deep within us
we long to know and experience more. The question asked
of us by Jesus takes us out of a space or frame of mind
where we are primarily in relationship just with ourselves,
to a space and frame of mind where we begin a genuine
relationship with God. In this chapter we explore this move
to relationship with God, our desire and our reluctance to
take this step, and what this move means as part of our
continuous conversion.

Between step one and step two: we love ourselves for ourselves; we love God for what he gives us

Following St Bernard's structure of the four steps, the move
from the first step of love to the second is about moving
from loving oneself for our own sake to loving God also for
our own sake. St Bernard, writing this in the twelfth century, understood that the movement towards letting God
into our lives, and then the progression to loving him,

begins when we see that we can get something from this. Human nature does seem predictable in this characteristic. St Bernard recognised that we begin by loving God for our own needs and advantage. In this way metaphorically we have one foot still in step one and the other taking a stride towards step two, but there is a movement – and a space has opened within us. St Bernard understood that no matter how we are or behave, we are loved by God who gives us good things, but it needs this opening within our own being before we can realise this. He writes that if we are subject to suffering and repeated difficulties, and because of these we turn towards God and experience some consolation and relief, then once we have had this experience we begin to appreciate and love God's actions within us.

This opening of our horizons to God also influences our relationship with other people. St Bernard thought that then perhaps we can shift from seeing others as only meeting our own needs, to having a sense of their needs. In other words, there is a possibility that we can start to feel real empathy and compassion for others. According to St Bernard, as we begin to share and care for other people we are acknowledging God in those other people. The Quaker tradition fits easily alongside this, the 'awareness of the Light that is in us all' and the query 'Do you respect that of God in everyone?'[1] As we move from self to recognition of the other we are also finding God.

'What are you looking for? ... Come and see'

When Jesus asks the disciples, 'What are you looking for?' they ask him as teacher, Rabbi, 'Where are you staying?' Jesus' answer is 'Come and see.' Jesus invites the two men to come and spend time with him. The narrative lets us know what happened: 'They came and saw where he was staying, and they remained with him that day. It was about four o'clock in the afternoon' (John 1:39). This was the relationship that was about to transform their lives and it had just begun.

Melvyn Matthews describes the experience of this transformation as a sudden falling into a black hole, an immediate realisation of grace, and the awareness they could be free, 'indeed quite simply, they were free'. He writes that the story is really

> a story about how a group of friends found themselves, saw their true selves suddenly, and were energised to really be, to really be who they were, beyond and above all that they ought, or thought they ought, to be – it's about their calling as people ... being surprised, being set free in the presence of Jesus, free to realize that he was more than they thought he was and that they too could be more than they had thought.

Melvyn Matthews reminds us that 'the immense, terrifying freedom-giving reality' of God is always very close to each one of us, 'nearer than breathing, closer than hands and feet'.[2] We need to make the turn towards him – he is there.

If we too, like the disciples, move to opening ourselves to relate to God, we are turning away from our self-preoccupation and self-love to notice and respond to God. If we answer the question about what we are looking for with another question that begins a relationship, then the final part of the sequence is that we too need to 'come and see' in the sense that we need to try this friendship out. Therefore the move towards step two is a move to the recognition of God's presence in our lives and the personal relationship that can then develop.

What does it mean to be in such a relationship with God? It means to be in a state of conscious connection with him. This involves a giving out and a taking in. It is as essential and natural as breathing. One of the basic techniques in meditation is to watch and count the breath as a way of focusing our attention, but how do we consciously connect with God and how can we begin to be aware of God in our lives?

Brother Lawrence, a seventeenth-century French monk, describes a similar process to watching the breath, when he suggests almost that we can watch God. He found a way, and advocated it to others, of fixing ourselves firmly in the presence of God by conversing all the time with him without mystery or artificiality. This, he teaches, initially needs perseverance, but all that is needed is our realisation that God is intimately present within us, and so we can turn at every moment to him in 'unbroken communion'.[3] For most of us, approaching the second step of love, reading about this practice of unbroken communion, can seem over the top, much too much, and what on earth are we doing if we start talking to God all the time? It might be suitable for a seventeenth-century monk but in our present times people would judge us as having lost it.

So how do we approach relationship and connection with God with our weariness and Western cynicism? Perhaps our very spiritual impoverishment can give us an appetite to take a look, and, as is true of all times and people, relationships are initially encouraged by curiosity. Perhaps first of all we also have to acknowledge our mixed feelings and inner conflict about taking this step.

Recognising our mixed feelings about really relating to God

Turning away from ourselves and towards this second step of love, in other words beginning a relationship with God, involves understanding and managing our fears about letting go and losing control. For many people this can only happen when life has reached rock-bottom, or the feelings of despair seem never-ending – there's nothing left to lose. It is in those states of mind that we know our need of God, and, if so, are blessed. For those of us who just about function, more or less most of the time, the risk of the loss of our definite selfhood can sometimes feel too great, and so we defend against any connection with God. He might ask too much of us, or it might be too challenging, or involve becoming too different, and in ways we would not like. After all, sometimes it's bad enough fitting in with the demands and wishes of our friends, or parents, or partner, or children, or work colleagues – God could just be another demand – and what about me!

Even more painful can be our fear of a good and loving relationship with God. Perhaps we doubt that possibility, or worry that we might feel trapped and so doomed to be, or behave, in some stereotyped or prescribed way. After all feeling trapped in close relationships is a universal human fear, and can be a major problem. It can mean that we pursue an 'in or out' half-way-house policy – neither fully committed nor letting go entirely, all is compromise. It sounds rather like the Schopenhauer parable of the porcupines. A number of porcupines huddled together because they were cold, but found that they pricked each other with their quills and so drew apart again. They went on in this 'in and out' fashion till eventually they found a distance where they were not quite so cold, but also did not prick each other.[4] In other words, some form of closeness is managed, but at a cost to any real intimacy.

If we are like the porcupines in our relationship with God, and sometimes a bit interested, but more often not really, praying only when we need to, or want something, avoiding any commitment or openness even within ourselves, then the compromise position means that we are living below the full potentiality of our relationship with

God, and sometimes nothing much happens. After all, the disciples in the story went to see, and then they stayed. They wondered how Jesus lived – what was he doing – and where was he staying – what was his take on life – what sort of person was he and did he have anything that they wanted? He began to become the person who could offer possible answers to their questions. Perhaps their initial response was not particularly hopeful, but by the end of that day their commitment was made. If we can risk it, then God can become, as he did for Brother Lawrence, the transformational action in our lives.

Sometimes, however, it seems that we make this huge step – we turn to God in our searching, and try to see what a relationship with him might be like. Perhaps our steps are too tentative, or God's timing is not as we thought, and nothing much seems to change. Perhaps we are still attached to our old and own way of life, and are only going through the motions of the relationship. Augustine spoke about the experience of being swept up to God through God's beauty and power, but the next moment torn away from God by his (Augustine's) own weight.

Perhaps as we think that we are making this move towards loving God our will reasserts itself even more strongly. The move from step one to step two can include conflict between what we thought we were looking for, and what we are actually finding. Events happen, and things shift, and so we become more open to the possibility that life is not limited to our own perception. There can be intellectual doubts or an increasing sense of isolation or even loneliness, even among friends. Sometimes the way ahead remains unclear and requires more trust than we have. The contradiction is that we have to open ourselves to this transformational action, in other words to the work of grace through the spirit.

God as transformational action – the great change-maker

Once we open ourselves to a connection with God and his love, then we open ourselves to his transformational action and our life begins to alter. Etty Hillesum documents her first moves in opening up a relationship with God. She realises that she needs time, and decides to set aside half an hour each morning before work and to clear some inner space, 'So that something of "God" can enter you, and something of "Love", too … the love you can apply to small, everyday things.'[5]

The initial experiences of the love of God working in our lives can leave us feeling very excited and positive – a bit like the feeling of being in love. Johannes Jorgensen wrote in his diary about his early conversion experiences: 'I have a strange feeling of freedom, of buoyancy – as if I were a balloon, presently to soar above the world around it.' He begins to recognise the idea of 'an eternal order' with a guiding and sustaining power that he names as God the Almighty. With this comes the realisation, 'I am beginning to understand what it means: to be in need of grace.' With the first tentative moves to relationship with God, Johannes Jorgensen writes that he is now able to give thanks – to thank God for what he has given him, 'for the gentle hand by which I felt myself guided'. And he prays for redemption.[6]

Evelyn Underhill describes a retreat over a 'wonderful week', in an atmosphere of almost perpetual prayer, which paved the way for her to receive one of the major experiences of her life. In her words:

> The day after I came away, a good deal shaken but unconvinced, I was 'converted' quite suddenly once and for all by an overpowering vision which had no

specific Christian element but yet convinced me that the Catholic religion was true.[7]

The accounts that people give of their conversions are unique because each conversion takes place in a context peculiar and important to that person. Some conversions are immediate and overwhelming, and then override all our known ways of processing what happens to us. The conversion of St Paul would be the blueprint for this. However, the majority of conversions take place over time, and with much preparation and groundwork, though this may be largely unconscious. There is often a time delay so that some people only realise later what has happened to them. Therefore it may then be that the recognition and mental recording of each conversion is accessed within the person's particular mindset and predominant way of processing experiences. This takes us back to the idea of intellectual, emotional and moral conversions and for each of us one particular way being more accessible than another. If our attraction is towards the intellectual we may then adapt the experience to fit that, and so with the emotional and the moral. As one commentator noted, pure theological content of the experience never lies at the moment of change, the moment only exists retrospectively and after reflection.[8] We can read that Etty Hillesum documented the emotion of love as the beginnings of her conscious connection with God. Johannes Jorgensen quickly framed his emotional feeling of buoyancy within a philosophical structure, while Evelyn Underhill located her conversion firmly within the institutional framework of the Church. Our conversion is subjective, and that's what gives it such power. It is also what gives it such confirmation as an authentic moment of conscious connection with God's transformational action. It is the beginning of our genuine personal relationship with God.

'Each of us is at the centre of infinite and marvellous combinations'

So writes Leon Bloy who says that if God gave it to us to see the infinite and marvellous combinations – in other words the patterns and paths God makes in our lives – 'we would enter Paradise in a swoon of pain and delight'.[9] As we move towards step two we begin to understand that what happens in our lives, what is going on inside us, and in response to our prayer, is something 'much more profound than we realize. The life of prayer is an encounter with the ultimate hidden reality of God.'[10] In the process, our illusions are gradually stripped away and we let go of our false and idolatrous gods, what Melvyn Matthews refers to as 'our bloated requirements' – 'I want this' or 'I want to be this' and 'I want this to happen'.

As God opens our eyes and comes into our consciousness we move into the second step of love. This means that we begin to see things as they really are. Our disconnected longings and our searching for something rather than nothing, all our intimations of the unthought known are replaced by the power of God's transformational action, and also so much more than we had previously known. We now know what we are looking for, and we also now know that there is no option other than to see this, and stay with it, as did Brother Lawrence – wherever it takes us.

✷

CHAPTER SIX

The second step of love:
'We love God for what he gives us'

THE PATH OF CONTINUOUS CONVERSION in our orientation towards God is a lifetime's journey. If we understand St Bernard's steps of love as states of mind where we can recognise and are aware of our thoughts and actions, then it seems realistic that we often falter, stumbling backwards and forwards between step one and step two for some time. St Bernard reminds us that if our troubles increase, and we turn to God in growing frequency, then, as he meets our need time after time, we begin to appreciate his grace and also come to love God for his very nature. The differing aspects of the groundwork of conversion – the intellectual, emotional and moral – together begin to converge and pervade every part of our life. In other words, we are not just making a diary change and having a commitment on a Sunday, but rather we experience a reorientation of our very being. Our new identity is 'as a self in relationship … not so much in terms of a transformed, improved self but as a self – for perhaps the first time – in relationship with Another'.[1] In this chapter we explore the second step and all the accompanying development that takes place in us and around us. We also ponder on the over-used word 'love' – what do we really mean by love in our relationship with God?

47

St Bernard's second step of love

In this second step of love we become aware of something that is happening to us, something that is being given to us. What is it that we are given by God? St Bernard calls it 'God's gifts', and perhaps this means God's transformational action. St Bernard understood that as we experience God's gifts or God's action, especially in times of trouble, and experience some relief from our trouble or consolation, so we grow in gratitude and grace. If it happens that we frequently turn to God when we are in difficulty, and are released from the difficulty through God's grace, then we begin to love God for what he gives us and has done for us. St Bernard points out that we are still loving God for our own sake rather than for God's sake, but that the process of receiving what God gives to us, leads us in time to a recognition that, in St Bernard's words, turns even 'a heart of stone in a breast of iron'.[2] This recognition is what helps us to move to the third step of love where we love God because of who he is.

So what is it that happens to us when we receive God's grace and transformational action? How is it that our difficulties are resolved? How do we feel released from what has troubled us? Perhaps it is rather that through God's grace and action in us we are given strength enough to be sustained. Abbé de Tourville wrote over a century ago about how we realise to what a degree 'our Lord always gets us out of our difficulties, in spite of our anxieties, weaknesses, and failings, then we begin to acquire assurance and serenity even in the midst of our troubles'. If we can trust God to be with us, and to help us, then the difficulty feels less overwhelming and even perhaps more meaningful. With the certainty that comes from personal experience Abbé de Tourville writes, 'Our Lord is with us in all our troubles and always gives us sufficient help to carry us through.'[3]

Horizontal and vertical expansion

When we are self-preoccupied and limited to the first step of love, our horizons are seriously restricted. The edges of our world are defined by our needs, our projections and our perceptions. As we move through the steps of love the space around us opens up, and we become conscious of God. One psalmist puts it this way:

> The LORD is my chosen portion and my cup; you hold my lot.
> The boundary lines have fallen for me in pleasant places; I have a goodly heritage. (Psalm 16:5–6).

As space emerges apart from our self and our desires, so our horizons expand – we no longer own or define them for our own benefit. The content of the answers we previously used to give our life meaning are altering. Turning towards God, and recognising that we are in relationship with him, alters the established content, and so our conversion is also a horizontal conversion – whether predominantly intellectual, emotional or moral, all begin to develop. We have new answers to old questions that go beyond the horizontal limits with which we had previously structured our life. Together with the expansion of our horizontal boundaries is the shift in the states of our spiritual consciousness. Kathleen Raine describes these, following William Blake, as 'the vertical dimension' and as a scale of values: 'call it Jacob's Ladder, on which spirits of higher mental regions descend to earth, and on which we, from the realities of this world ascend in vision'. She is clear that by this she does not mean another world but rather the manner in which we experience this one.[4] These dimensions, both the horizontal and the vertical, are within us – in the beholder. This transforming and deepening divine power operates in this world. In the Irish eighth-century hymn we sing of seeing

49

through the eyes of God who is also the focus of our looking.

> Be thou my vision, O Lord of my heart;
> Naught be all else to me, save that Thou art
> Thou my best Thought, by day or by night,
> Waking or sleeping, Thy presence my light.

The last verse ends with

> Heart of my own heart, whatever befall,
> Still be my Vision, O Ruler of all.

Expansion in our spiritual consciousness begins to alter the way we see the world. We speak of throwing light on a situation, and seeing things in a new light. This is the divine action, and through it we begin to be different in our relationships with others, and to develop our view and our views.

It's life ... but not as we knew it

One of the interesting developments in the second step of love is that we gradually begin to understand and know who we really are. Strangely the discovery of God turns out to be also as much about discovering ourselves. As with any relationship we are inevitably affected, and the greater the amount of time we spend in the relationship, the greater the influence and impact on us. We may be wary of getting too close – and also wary of the alternative which is to be left in the cold – the dilemma of the porcupines again. Inevitably we bring with us into all our relationships, and especially so into our relationship with God, our template of previous relationships, and old fears of losing ourselves in another's needs, or feeling rejected if we step away. The extraordinary realisation that emerges as our relationship with God develops is that, unlike our human relationships, God is not in rivalry with us. There are complications, but they are different from human-to-human complications; for a start we are not dealing with another egoic structure.

One thing that we might discover quite early on is that we sometimes treat God as we do others – perhaps this is what step two of St Bernard's ladder of love is really about. We are treating God as if *he* exists to serve and respond to *our* needs and this of course links back to step one of love. Pope John XXIII writes about this in his autobiographical *Journey of a Soul*: 'until now I have always trifled with God, and God is not to be trifled with.'[5] This awareness of the depths of our neediness demands that we understand ourselves and our motivation in turning to God, and inevitably within that understanding we start to learn about humility. As we open ourselves to God and self-importantly present ourselves in this relationship, we are in fact beginning a long process of discovery about knowing ourselves as we really are. In this knowing we will move from centre stage to relocate God as the centre of our lives.

Seeing ourselves in a new light can be a painful process. Johannes Jorgensen, the Danish writer, had rather delighted in his conversion and what he had seen as his successful intellectual critiques and defence of God, but comes to understand that he seems incapable of real love, and thinks this true both in his professional and personal life. Without love or charity he feels as 'nothing'. 'And nothing is the opposite of *Being*, of God. Nothing is death, it is everlasting death.' This state of mind continues, and through his developing self-awareness Johannes Jorgensen begins a painful process of stripping away what he now sees as the illusion of his conversion.

In particular he reproaches himself for his relationship with his wife: 'I have been very *petty* and believed myself very great; very *cruel* and thought I was very kind; very crabbed and thought I was a suffering Christian spirit.' In the midst of the light of conversion he feels himself as a man of darkness. He writes: 'it was terrible to be I.'[6]

What does love mean?

In a similar way to Johannes Jorgensen, part of Thomas Merton's journey in relationship with God is a journey in developing his experience of what love means. When Thomas Merton spends Holy Week in 1941 on retreat at Gethsemani he reads and reflects on St Bernard's four steps of love. His monastic life with the Trappists is grounded in the Cistercian teaching on love, and he reflects and comments on the text of the four steps of love in much of his writing. The monastic life, according to this understanding, is about learning to love – or, as Thomas Merton puts it, 'a school of charity', 'you came to the monastery', he writes, 'to learn, or rather relearn, the love whose seeds were implanted in your very nature'.[7] Contemplative life is then a life of love.

Understanding that just quoting or even explaining medieval texts wasn't enough for contemporary readers, he wrote in his journal in December 1957, after 16 years in the monastery:

> Love is the only answer. But medieval talk about love solves nothing. What does love mean today? What is its place in the enormous dimensions of the modern world? We have to love in a new way and with a new attitude and I suppose perhaps the first thing to do is to admit I do not know the meaning of love in *any* context – ancient or new.

Like Johannes Jorgensen, Thomas Merton acknowledges that in the light of Jesus Christ he does not know what love really means. In his writings he draws on traditional sources, but frames these within his thoughts on alienation and authenticity, personalism and individualism, all resulting from the tendency to turn love towards the self rather than towards God. If we can grow in the light of God's love and reciprocate God's love, we can gradually open ourselves to loving others in the way we now have been loved. In other words, God teaches us the real meaning of love and how to love. A few months after the realisation that he did not know what love meant Thomas Merton has a seminal experience of love when on a rare journey into the town from the monastery.

> Yesterday, in Louisville, at the corner of 4th and Walnut, suddenly realised that I loved all the people and that none of them were, or could be, totally alien to me. As if waking from a dream – the dream of my separateness, of the 'special' vocation to be different.[8]

As we move away from our own special self-importance and the self-importance of our conversion we understand better our connection to others, and the implications of the deepening relationship to God. Who is it that we are in relationship with? We are not in relationship with a concept, nor with a series of teachings, nor a moral code – but with all of these and something deeply personal and so much more, something that is neither describable nor limited by our thoughts.

Beginnings of new consciousness

As we begin to acknowledge this tentative connection to God, so we try to frame our experiences through words. In the Bible we can read, and then later read again and again with deeper understanding, about the experiences of others and also the direct teachings of Jesus Christ. If we meditate and reflect on a text we can sometimes reach an impasse when we continue to limit our understanding through the predominant aspect such as the intellectual, the emotional or the moral. In other words, we do not know how to involve the whole of ourselves in what is happening. The other parts of us may be neglected potentialities. How can this clinging to aims and attitudes that are too narrow and too timid be remedied?

Christopher Bryant suggests one way is constantly to admit our insufficiency and the inadequacy of the particular attitude that we have. He suggests that we also need to develop the other weaker parts. It makes sense that initially we use the part of our self that is the most developed and with which we are most familiar. So, for example, if we are an intellectual person we may be drawn to be with God through reasoned meditation. If we are more emotional then we might more easily practise affective prayer. The more morally driven person may respond through social action or particular behaviours. As we understand how one-sided or even unbalanced we are, we turn to God. In one way we are asking God to help us come to terms with the rejected parts of our self – we are asking him to make us whole. As we do this so we understand our need of God. As Christopher Bryant writes, 'As the little conscious ego makes its act of no confidence in its unaided efforts it opens doors through which Light and Power will flow from within.'

He sees this as the growth to maturity which also goes together with the growth to self-awareness, 'which ... is the gateway to a deeper awareness of God'.[9] Perhaps the changes that then take place are dramatic, and could even be viewed as too much of a swing in another direction. Sometimes what seems to happen is that as we struggle to see ourselves in the light of Christ, so we also drop the part of our self that we presented to the world and which was apparently who we were. In other words, the alterations and adjustments that take place through continuous conversion can be seen as the emergence of the person's fundamental nature, and who they are meant to be. Both St Francis and Charles de Foucauld are examples of people who changed from a life of richness and sensuality to a life of asceticism and prayer.

It is in this context in this second step of love that we can begin to wonder and get a sense of God's great commandments of how we are to live. As the lawyer asks Jesus in Matthew 22:36–37, 'Teacher, which commandment in the law is the greatest?' Jesus said to him, 'You shall love the Lord your God with all your heart, and with all your soul, and with all your mind.' We are instructed to love God with every part of us. And Jesus adds the second commandment which tells us to genuinely love one another in the same way that we can genuinely love our self.

The continuous conversion that follows our journey along the steps of love leads to deep developments based on the fundamental values of the way we see the world. Following Christ is a change of direction intellectually, emotionally and morally. In the second step of love we begin this personal revolution as we start to turn away from self towards God. The moral changes are particularly strong as the gradual recognition of the reality of what God's love means begins to demand that we behave and respond to others differently. This process in itself demands of us a certain self-transcendence – in other words, we turn from our self and move beyond our self.

The second question that Jesus puts to us can help us think further about the second step of love and this is explored in the next chapter.

CHAPTER SEVEN

The second question:
'But who do you say that I am?'

CERTAINLY STRANGE THINGS HAPPEN when we put ourselves in the hands of God. One of the strangest things is that in this second step of love, as we realise the extent to which God is with us, so we begin to turn our attention towards him, and therefore away from ourselves. This then leads us to the inevitable question: who or what is it that I am turning to? Jesus Christ asks each of us, 'Who do *you* say that I am?' He doesn't ask us this in terms of doctrine – it's not an abstract intellectual answer that's needed; he doesn't ask us this in terms of morality and behaviour – the 'shoulds and the oughts' of our conduct; but he does ask this of us personally – it seems an emotional question that seeks a subjective answer.

'Who do you say that I am?' Who am I for you?

The context for this question which is found in Matthew's gospel (16:15) is the recording of the establishment of a new community where Jesus' true identity is acknowledged and which will become the focus of God's activity in history. The event is triggered by the rejection of Jesus by so many in Israel including the leaders.[1] Jesus asks his disciples what other people think of him, and the general view is that he is seen as a prophet. Jesus then personalises the question, prefixed with a 'but'. It is Peter's answer, 'You are the Messiah, the Son of the living God', which leads to Jesus' own revelation of Peter's destiny. As we each come to recognise who Jesus is for each of us, so our own path towards him becomes clearer.

George Fox, the inspiration behind the Society of Friends, writes in his Journal in 1647 about his search for someone who, as he describes it, 'could speak to my condition'. He had turned away from the priests and the established church and 'walked mournfully about by myself'. At the depths of his despair he heard a voice leading him to a direct relationship with Jesus Christ. He recognises that Jesus Christ is the one, 'who enlightens, and gives grace, and faith, and power ... And this I knew experimentally.'[2] George Fox knew this in his very being and through his own experience. He was given values and qualities that altered his life, and indeed the very boundaries of who he thought he was. One way of understanding our answer to Jesus' second question is that it is part of the way by which we become the person who we are meant to be. In our contemporary Western context we hear the question that Jesus asks us against a backdrop where belief in a personal relationship with Jesus Christ is seen largely as irrelevant, and if at all as an embarrassment. Nonetheless, the question is for us here and now, and one that we are drawn to reflect on throughout our spiritual journeying. Our individual experience is part of the ongoing new community and, within that, part of God's activity both in history and outside historical time.

There will always be more to experience as we move through the steps of love, and we return to reflect on the implications of this question as our faith evolves. Laurence

Freeman sees this question as key: to ask who Jesus is implies 'who he is for me, to me, and in relation to me' and then 'who we are as well'.[3] This is much more important than who he was historically, and takes us beyond moulding Jesus to fit with our own prejudices and opinions. Although the question is asked of each of us and requires our personal answers, it is also a question that unites us with one another. This is because our reflections link us with the universal experience of spiritual searching, and eventually we are told that our answer will lead us into the reality of the divine presence and the community of true faith.

Unknowing one's false self

Thinking about the question that Jesus asks us leads to thinking about who we really are, especially in relation to him. The question 'How are you?', which we ask so casually of each other, is the question that then needs to be turned back on our self – 'How am I? Really and honestly: *How am I?*' Part of not knowing the answer to Jesus' question to us, or finding partial answers that then alter as we evolve, means that we also deepen our perception of *who* we are. In other words, as we explore our inscape, which is the inner geography that is partly long established and partly recently constructed, we start to let go of the self that we have constructed and our manufactured answer to the questions 'How am I?' and 'Who am I?' If we can let go or 'unknow' our false self, we open up more space around us, and this can be space for God's transformational action. As Jeremy Taylor wrote: 'There should be in the soul halls of space, avenues of leisure, and high porticos of silence, where God walks.'[4]

If we start to let go of our constructed self then we may find other aspects of our self emerging. One contemporary

58

hymn asks whether if Jesus calls our name we can love the hidden part of our self, and in so doing suppress our fear and become someone different.[5]

The hidden parts of our self may be parts that we have rejected or repressed, or perhaps just aspects that did not fit with the demands of our everyday life, or the way we felt we were supposed to be. The constructed false self then begins to become increasingly irrelevant and even foreign to the way we are now feeling. Sometimes the self we have constructed has been a way of looking after a more vulnerable hidden part of our self. It is the real or true part of our being that is responding to Jesus' invitation to 'come and see' and to find out who he may be for us, and who we are meant to be for him. One way of unknowing one's false self is to begin to lessen our investment in ourselves. We grow closer to God and experience this subjectively, but there is of course a danger of becoming stuck in examining and analysing all our feelings, which then is another form of self-love or even spiritual narcissism. In other words there is a danger of turning away from God towards another apparently more interesting part of our personality – 'what an interesting spiritual person I am'. The fascinating feelings that change with every situation are in the end another dimension to the false self.

Evelyn Underhill writes bluntly in a letter of spiritual direction,

> What you happen to be *feeling* at the moment, does not matter in the least. Do – *do* try and be more objective in your religion. Try to see yourself less as a complex individual, and more as a quite ordinary scrap of the universe.

She urges the move away from self-love to a disinterest in the self and increasing interest in loving God. This includes not dwelling on one's failings and frailty: 'All this preoccupation with your own imperfection is not humility, but an insidious form of spiritual pride.'[6] Jesus' question is an invitation to move beyond the ego-self and connect with our true being.

Every time we become involved in a healthy relationship we have to relinquish part of our self, and if we have a healthy relationship with God it is the same. In some ways, 'we must become unrecognisable to ourselves in order to see who he [Jesus Christ] really is'.[7] It is only when we have created space around ourselves and let go of our self-interest that we can begin to know the answer to the question. Perhaps we also need to begin to let go of thinking and analysing it all.

> I would not be *thinking about* God's love, but just have a habitual awareness of this fact, that whether you think about it or not, everything will be taken care of, and hence what I really mean by it is not thinking about yourself and not trying to figure everything out.[8]

Knowing the answer

As we recognise the expansion of the horizontal and vertical dimension in our selves so we realise that any answer to this question cannot be final. Answers stop dead our curiosity, and in that way they kill off our questioning. 'Experience brings it home to you that you can give what we call "answers" but they are really space stoppers.' If we then believe the answer we come up with, there is no possible expansion of consciousness. However, if we cannot answer, 'you widen the breach, this nasty hole where one hasn't any knowledge at all', and this can sometimes lead to anxiety. What does it mean for us not to know the answer to Jesus' question? There is, I think, a fear in not knowing, but there is also a deep fear of knowing the truth: 'The fear of knowing the truth can be so powerful that the doses of truth are lethal.'[9] One reason for such apprehension would be because the next step of love, the third step, asks us to let go of the primacy of our self and turn our full attention towards God. If we can manage not to stop the space opened by this question with an instant answer (and even if we answer as Peter did we are left uncertain as to what that answer means for us), then we are making ourselves available to the transformational action of God which will lead us to the truthful answer.

The type of knowing (or rather not-knowing) where our reflections on the question begin to lead us in new directions is not about intellectual thinking; nor is it based on moral certainties, and it is not vacillating emotion. It is not about thought, but rather about conscious awareness. It is a form of knowing from within that can make use of all these three perspectives, but is also more than that. Such knowing is illuminated by grace – the 'more than our selves'. The experience of loving God for what he gives us contributes to the internalisation of our personal knowledge of God. Sometimes we are helped to find words for this from the Bible and from the liturgy. This way of knowing is not objective, but a partial perspective which depends on our subjective situation, but not on self-interest. Yet we also have access to the subjective experiences of others, some of which have taken on an authority over and above others and become doctrine. All that we can access we can make use of to assess and integrate our own experiences. This is then an embodied knowledge – an internalised knowing from within, but framed in the context of the universal experience of spiritual searching. The poet Robert Browning described it well,

> ... and 'to know'
> Rather consists in opening out a way.

One place where the question is answered

One place where we are both given to by God and also learn to answer Jesus Christ's question is at the Eucharist: 'In a crumb of bread the whole mystery is.'[10] The Eucharist is the way in which many Christians over the centuries have drawn near to God, and been fed spiritual food and gained spiritual strength. It also contributes to reminding each of us about the whole life of the Church, and that we are included in the new community that recognises who Jesus Christ is and what he means for them.

It is in the Eucharist that Jesus Christ gives himself. It is a gift outside of time and for ever, a perpetual sacrifice offered by an eternal priest. Christ as the truth is present with us, and connects with our deepest self. At the point of consecration Christ himself speaks the words in the first person through the mouth of the priest, and so is both sacrificed and the one who sacrifices.

What do we need to do with our self when we participate in the Eucharist? Most advice is that we need to try to set aside our thinking, our worries and our needs, and direct all our psychic energy on the sacrament. In other words, we begin the struggle to keep our mind present with Christ. This then employs our will, so as our thoughts inevitably wander we try to bring our mind back to a still space. This is also called the practice of 'mindfulness'.

> What is called for is not intense concentration, with a knitting of the brows, but, rather, the opposite, an awakening of the mind without fixing it anywhere, the quietness of pure attention ... our minds unclouded by egoistical emotions, and so made more aware of God Himself.[11]

Evelyn Underhill writes: 'through his self-giving God comes into the soul whether we know it or not. Holy

Communion is one of the great ways we actualize this and also give *ourselves* in turn, to be used in the Divine work of redeeming the world.' From her experience as both someone who didn't attend communion and then who did, she wrote, 'There is no doubt at all left in my own mind as to what is the simplest and most direct channel through which grace comes to the soul.'[12] Carl Jung, in his analysis of the symbolism of the mass, writes that it makes visible something that is eternal outside of time and space. It is where and when, 'the eternal character of the single divine experience becomes evident … as if a window or a door had been opened upon that which lies beyond space and time'.[13] It is a moment where, if we can bear it, we can be truly alive and open to the third step of love where we love God for himself.

Robert Johnson, a Jungian analyst, had a period in his life when he stayed and worked in a Benedictine monastery running a therapy practice and retreat centre. He describes an experience when walking through a street he heard a demand in his head: 'Now make up your mind: either everything in the world is the body and blood of Christ, or nothing is. Make up your mind.' He remembers that this was such a shock that he can still recall the external scene vividly. For him it was a terrible, and at the same time wonderful, moment. As he says, he knew the answer immediately, but he didn't know what to do with it. If he said that nothing was he would die immediately from a lack of meaning in his life: 'it was clear that Christ must be everything. But how could I live with that truth? It seemed too big to take in. I have been struggling since with the implication of that vision.'[14]

If we begin to move our false constructed self to one side then we have room for God. To live in the light of the Eucharist seems to mean the possibility of beginning to live with stillness and a spaciousness that allows us to be present and aware, without being dominated by what happens in our illusory self, with our all too human fears and our transient needs.

Practical suggestions linked to the second step of love and the second question

Exercise 1: My life story

Meister Eckhart wrote that no one can know God who has not first known himself or herself. Therefore, we need to know who we are before we can look beyond that.

- Write your life story in exactly 100 words – but with a few restrictions: keep to the present tense and keep to words of only one syllable. For example, you might want to say, 'I was born in London', but instead you would need to say, 'I am born in the big smoke'.
- Give yourself a time limit of a maximum of 15 minutes. How simple can you get it? What do you feel about the different times in your life to date? Can you remember what you felt then and what you feel about it now?

You will use this life story later so keep hold of it.

Exercise 2: Who is God? Who is Jesus?

> To see God, as He appears in Jesus, and to cast oneself upon Him, is to be delivered from the fear of things, and very especially from the fear of tasks which scare us by their size. We get back our nerve as we look at Him.[15]

How can we develop authenticity in how we see God and how we see that he appears in Jesus?

Part 1

Take two minutes to write down whatever words come into your mind in response to the word 'God'. Then do the same for the word 'Jesus'.

Don't think about it or censor anything. It doesn't matter how silly the words seem and there will always be paradoxes and contradictions. There's no right or wrong – this is about a process of discovery.

When you have finished, look at the words you have listed. Is there any pattern to them? For example, do the words describe God in terms of a monarch, or from the vocabulary of war, or the law courts? Is there any link to creation? What about the name 'Jesus'? Are the words taken from personal experience? Are there particularly feminine or masculine qualities that are listed? Do the words give the impression that God is beyond knowledge? How many words are linked to knowledge of Bible stories and accounts of Jesus' life? Are there childish residues in either of the descriptions?[16]

Part 2

The second part of this exercise is about gathering up our projections – this is a process of redemption.

Projection is when we give away part of our soul – we (without knowing it) 'drape' part of ourselves onto someone or something else. This can happen particularly powerfully with God and Jesus. Why would we do this? Well, it's because the other person or concept or thing has some quality that is very much like a part of our self we *don't* yet know. That acts as a hook on which we can drape that part of our self. We can usually work it out when we have a very strong over-reaction – a more than usual feeling which can be either positive or negative. In our spiritual life recognising this is a gift – an act of grace as it gives us a chance to see that part and take it back. We can learn from this more about who we are, especially the hidden parts. When we suspect that we are projecting (no matter where or on what), we need to examine what is happening and spend some time with that positive or negative part of ourselves and take it back. We need to withdraw the projection and try to integrate it with the rest of ourselves. We need to own it and by doing so we redeem it.[17]

So, look again at your lists of words about God and Jesus. Can you see some qualities that evoke especially strong feelings – especially if they are negative – e.g. a punishing, vengeful God, a crushed, guilt-making Jesus. Where do these words really come from? How much are we distorting our experience of God and Jesus? It's also useful to hold onto this idea of redeeming our projections and be aware when we are projected onto when we are with others – perhaps especially in religious groups. Owning our projections is part of an authentic way of living.

Suggestions: ideas for sharing

Honest with God

Bring your feelings to Jesus and really feel and own them in his presence: tell God as he appears in Jesus about how you are feeling. This might be a useful way of beginning some prayer time. For example:

- I am feeling excited and hopeful about prayer and I own that feeling in the light of your presence.
- I am feeling lost and disillusioned in my relationship with you and I own that feeling in the light of your presence.

We might as well be honest with God – after all, he knows what we're feeling anyway.

Breaking through to the mystery

We can know about theology, we can read about the experiences of other people, but it is important that we can get through to the experience ourselves. God is calling us to direct knowledge of him – subjectively. We are seeking God within our self – within a part of the self that is potentially available to God's personal call. In other words, we have to find our way to becoming ever closer and in some way becoming as like Jesus as we can; this is what gives us knowledge and it is what Jesus wants from us and to give to us. It is from this relationship with Jesus that we can begin to identify with him. One way to do that is to include him in our life (just as Brother Lawrence shows us) – to make space not just by reading or thinking about him but by including him in the depths of our psyche. He becomes part of how we think, behave and react. Jesus becomes part of our very in-breath and out-breath, and the first person that we turn to in our inner life. It is a sharing of the best and the worst of us in the understanding that despite everything we are loved.

Prayers

1. Jesus, help me to uncover the person that you are calling me to become; help me to know you in my true self. Amen.
2. Father, you know the hardness of our hearts and the secrets we would hide; purify us in the fire of your Spirit and fill us with the gift of your love that we may walk in your ways for ever. Amen.[18]
3. Try to write your own prayer for this second step and second question. Here is an outline plan:

   - decide what you want to happen;
   - decide what can bring this about;
   - decide on a relative clause (e.g. your Son Jesus Christ revealed himself to the lost and poor);
   - find an appropriate opening and ending.

(Tips: don't pretend or lie to God; avoid cliché or overly religious language; say it as is natural to you.)[19]

Thought: story

A Hasidic tale is told about Rabbi Susya who was very ill, and at his advanced age it was clear that he would not live much longer.

He was very sad, and told a friend about his approaching death in gloomy tones. The friend said, 'Well are you afraid that God will think you didn't turn out like Moses?' The Rabbi replied, 'Oh no, I'm afraid God will think I didn't turn out like Susya.'[20]

CHAPTER EIGHT

The third step of love:
'We love God for himself'

IN THIS CHAPTER on the third step we initially consider the ever-present pull back to self-interest. However, if we are to love God for himself then our entire being will shift from having the self at the centre towards placing God at the centre. This inevitably implies a surrendering of control.

The movement towards and away from God

The third step of love according to St Bernard is about loving God for himself. This surely means that we begin to move from a state of mind based predominantly on fear about ourselves to one of concern and compassion for others. Yet it also still seems to be characterised by alternating between a love for God and a pull back towards self-interest. Etienne Gilson writes that it 'is in this state that the soul remains for the longest time, nor indeed can she [our soul] ever wholly emerge from it in this life'.[1] It is in this very alternation between love for God and for our self that the move for freedom is located. We may long to turn more fully to God, but often can be pulled back by fear into self-interested love.

There is a wonderful example of this alternation in the story of Peter, the disciple, in Matthew 14:22–34, and of his attempt to be like Jesus and walk on water. We imagine from the account that Peter has been in a place of excitement and wonder since meeting Jesus. On this particular night, the disciples have gone ahead of Jesus, crossing the lake in the boat and leaving him to pray alone. Overnight the water becomes very rough, and the boat is far from land. Jesus walks to the boat on the water. In the strange half light before dawn the disciples fear that Jesus is a ghost. Immediately Jesus reassures them, 'Take heart, it is I; do not be afraid.' Peter, relieved, enthusiastic and perhaps also in touch with some aggression after the fear has subsided, sets out to imitate Jesus and walk on the water.

The symbolism of what happens can be understood in different ways. We can read it as an analogy of the 'surface' faith that we can easily identify with and find instantly attractive. When we, like Peter, realise the deeper implications of what we are doing, he and we panic and begin to sink. As we start to acknowledge Jesus, we, like Peter, can feel frightened by the otherness of spiritual power – 'what on earth am I doing walking on water, or some equally unfamiliar behaviour?', and also think we are not worthy to receive it. Another way of reading into the symbolism of Peter's sinking is to look at his fear of becoming different. Perhaps what he is doing as he feels the power of the elements is a projection of his fear and panic at all that has altered in his life. It is hard to acknowledge that we might be frightened of good things that happen to us, and good developments in our life. It is even harder to acknowledge our lack of control and our surrender to something that we cannot validate or check out in conventional ways and that other people may not understand. We, like Peter, at these times need to call out to Jesus for his help – 'Lord, save me!'

In the gospel account, Peter, as he sinks into the water,

inevitably finds himself again in a place where his own anxieties predominate – he is back at the first step of love and totally self-preoccupied. He is naturally only concerned for his own safety and self – he has stopped looking towards Jesus with love. Instead, he is transfixed by the power of the waves and the wind. He is very afraid for his own survival. He then moves on to the second step of love when he calls out to Jesus, loving him for what he can give him. This state of mind is contrasted with the third step of love, one where only love and concern for Jesus are to the fore. As Peter sets out to walk on the water towards Jesus, he moves from the state of relatedness back to a state of mind where he becomes cut off from his relationship with Jesus. The other aspect of this story is that Jesus, because he is more than our selves, can cut through this – he both understands and is more powerful than our transient states of mind or wherever we might be on the four steps of love. In the story he reaches out to Peter, and Peter is reconnected to Jesus. In our relationship with God things are 'done to us' – despite ourselves.

One of the things we can learn from others is that there is continual movement between the frames of mind associated with the four steps of love. Sadly it seems that it's not a case of arriving at the next step and staying there – so we can 'note' our spiritual progress – but rather that we have to be ever open to what happens and our responses. Perhaps the spiral path of the spiritual journey can sometimes also threaten to lead us back down and away from God.

Growing closer to God

St Bernard is more hopeful when he writes that as we approach God more often, so our intimacy with God grows. As we 'come and see' and remain with the experience that we are having in the relationship with God, so we begin to appreciate his presence. In other words, we start to love the experience of closeness with God in all of our ordinary everyday life, and this becomes more important than what he has given us. St Bernard puts it in the style of his time:

> This intimacy moves us to taste and to discover how sweet the Lord is. Tasting God's sweetness entices us more to pure love than does the urgency of our own needs … We say to our flesh, 'Now we love God not because of your needs, for we have tasted and know how sweet the Lord is.'

St Bernard continues that this state of mind leaves us free to follow the commandment to love our neighbour – for if we love God then we will love everything that belongs to God. The love involved is free and involves our actions, 'it renders what is received'. Perhaps this means that what we are given generously we can begin to give to others, because it is God himself who is the focus of our attention. We are then really loving others as we have been loved ourselves – not in a possessive or competitive manner, but

> seeking in turn not what is our own but what belongs to Christ, the same way Christ sought not what was his but what was ours, or rather, ourselves. He so loves who says: 'Confess to the Lord for he is good'. One who confesses to the Lord, not because the Lord is good to him or her but because the Lord is good, truly loves God for God's sake and not for one's own benefit.[2]

Our orientation shifts further

The third step of love may involve many oscillations between self-interest and looking to God, but it seems as if underneath there is probably a radical shift taking place. If

73

we love God for himself – even if just for some of the time – then we are gradually coming to realise God's presence in all of life. We are experiencing that he loves us. With this comes the radical shift in orientation. In other words, as we grow closer to God and realise that something is happening to us, we can begin to relinquish our fear and love the experiences we have when we are freed of our anxiety and worry. As we 'come and see' so we move to 'taste and see'. As St Bernard puts it, this intimacy with God becomes more attractive to us than the earlier phase and the dead-end cul-de-sac of self-preoccupation.

Gerard Hughes, writing after a particularly anxious time on his walk to Jerusalem, puts it like this:

> I looked at the candle in the darkness and recognised the darkness in all the bewilderment, numbness, frustration, helplessness and anxiety I had experienced …
>
> The light came into the darkness and I felt the joy of it, an inner certainty in all my uncertainty, a hope when everything seemed hopeless, an assurance that all manner of things will be well and that Christ is greater than all my stupidity and sinfulness. I knew then that I was caught up in something far greater than my mind can ever grasp.[3]

We love God as we experience him loving us and guiding us, but we struggle to articulate to those who are sceptical (and to the sceptical part of us) what this is and what this means. Yet as the experiences of this intimacy (whether it is when good things are happening to us or bad things) become part of us, so we can let go of the need to reduce, rationalise, define and own what is happening. Then we might be able sometimes just to let it all happen.

Making ourselves vulnerable

Perhaps, above all, this third step of love is about being open and vulnerable. We are no longer unclear about what we are looking for as in the first step, nor are we seeing what we can get out of our relationship with God as in the second step. The stripping lessens our reliance on external appearances, and inevitably opens us to the spiritual spaces within us. If we are seeing ourselves differently we may also feel freer to acknowledge our wrongdoing, our need of and our dependency on God, but this time, unlike earlier in the steps of love, we may now feel able to trust God more.

The psalmist who wrote Psalm 143, one of the penitential psalms, puts it like this in verses 6 and 8: 'I stretch out my hands to you; my soul thirsts for you like a parched land.' There is confidence that the need will be met and the prayer answered: 'Let me hear of your steadfast love in the morning, for in you I put my trust.' The psalmist also asks for guidance: 'Teach me the way I should go, for to you I lift up my soul.' The image here is one of looking up for guidance from a place of openness and vulnerability. We are beginning to see ourselves in relation to God and acknowledge our lack without him and our need for him to help us. Again in verse 10: 'Teach me to do your will, for you are my God. Let your good spirit lead me on a level path.' In other words, the movement is towards 'let it be with me according to your word' (Luke 1:38).

Surrendering control

Moving to a space where we are increasingly oriented to God and his love for us, we learn to love him for himself. The whole process of letting go of self is the letting go of the illusory idea that we are in control. This can also happen when we allow ourselves to bring our fear out of the darkness and into the light. We are frightened of so many things and mostly to do with losing control. It may be connected to what other people are or do to us; what happens to us or to those we are close to; a fear of sickness, and for all of us inevitably a fear of pain and of death. If we can acknowledge our terror and reveal it to Jesus, this is the beginning of surrendering control to God, whom we can freely love for who he is and what he does for us and to us.

In June 1906 Raissa Maritain wrote:

> My God I am here before thee
> I crumble into nothing before thee
> I adore thy greatness
> My need is immense
> Have pity on me.[4]

The following year, in January 1907, she became seriously ill and received the last rites of the Church, which she experienced as a new baptism, and which, she wrote, flooded her with 'grace and peace' and 'the joy of suffering'. Her bodily recovery was 'sudden and undeniable'. She offered to God what she always referred to thereafter as 'the total gift of herself' ('l'abandon total de soi').[5] In her Journal she records that she still continued to experience fear and worry, but was able to observe these emotional responses and place them in the context of her life with Christ. In other words, these inevitable human emotions still happened, and she clearly felt them in her suffering, but there was now a larger background where they could be placed and accepted. The fear and pain that she felt was no longer everything, but part of the bigger picture. In her Rule of Life Raissa wrote:

> Accept all as coming from God
> Do all for God
> Offer all to God.[6]

※

CHAPTER NINE

The third question:
'Do you know what I have done
to you?'

The question, and understanding the foot-washing

The question asked by Jesus Christ that resonates with this third step of love is found in John 13:12: 'After he had washed their feet, had put on his robe, and had returned to the table, he said to them, "Do you know what I have done to you?"' In this simple action and service, Jesus tells the disciples that he has shown his love for them and also, the only time it is said in the gospels, given them an example of how they are to serve others and return the love. The example is clearly not that we should all be literally washing each other's feet, but a symbolic action of compassion, service and acceptance of each other and of that of Christ in each other. The question is also an all-pervasive one, and beyond its immediate context it is asked about the influence of Jesus in our lives. The phrase *'done to you'* stands out – this is something that has begun to happen to our very being. The question asked includes our recognition of the unique way that God operates in each of our lives. The question and our answer are about acknowledging Jesus Christ. This is not only about what Jesus has done *for* us, but also about the recognition of what Jesus does *to* us. Joel Giallanza frames the question in this way:

> 'Do you know what I have done to you?' since you have been with me and I with you – during all that has happened (will happen) to us since the beginning of my ministry? The disciples, in this larger context, must reflect on all that has taken place. They must begin to see Jesus' life and ministry as a single incarnate expression of the Father's love. Jesus is the Exemplar, the one to whom all Christian lives must point.[1]

The question is placed within the context of the last supper, and the betrayal and death of Christ. As we are moved to love God for what he is, we are asked not only to follow Jesus' example in terms of our relationship to others, but also in terms of sacrificial death in our relationship with God. The symbolism of the foot-washing ritual and ceremony is linked with Jesus' sacrificial death. There are clear associations to the sacrament of Christian baptism, and both forms of cleansing are seen as symbolically transformative for both are a welcome into the community and company of God.

In the dialogue with Peter about whether or not he allows Jesus to wash his feet, it seems that the washing is part of the ritual needed for Peter to become 'wholly' clean, and so to have a special inheritance or place with Jesus. Peter will understand and follow some time afterwards, and so through the washing comes to a liminal state of transformation. His understanding is incomplete, but he is on the edge of knowing. This in a sense categorises the deepening aspects of the third step of love. It takes us to the edge of true awareness. In the gospel account, part of Peter's incomprehension is how Jesus, as master and teacher, should put himself in such a humble position as a foot-washer. Jesus reverses the usual master–servant expectations, and once again offers an unworldly example of such relationships.

Any relationship with Jesus Christ carries all the elements of the other relationships we have with one another, but often the qualities are turned around and given a different meaning. We move in our relationship with God into the depths of the vertical dimension. The question, 'Do you know what I have done to you?' in the context of the action of foot-washing seems to suggest that, as we relinquish control to God, so we are no longer master of our own house. Yet the master who is now at home within us is also our servant, who prepares us both for service and a true meeting with God.

Finding the Great Companion

Much has happened since searching for what we want for ourselves with the question 'What are you looking for?', followed by the acknowledgement that we are in relationship with Jesus Christ, with the question 'Who do *you* say that I am?', and further on in the relationship with God where something has happened to us, almost outside our conscious awareness, with the question 'Do you know what I have done to you?' What was the unthought known has gradually become a conscious presence through the transformational action of God. Perhaps it is only later that we can see that we have been deeply affected, and that what was dimly guessed at, and then glimpsed, has become increasingly important in our lives. Our spiritual landscape has altered, and we are increasingly conscious of much that was buried in the spiritual unconscious.

Traditionally those who are searching for God seek spiritual direction from someone else. Nowadays, the advice and support given is rarely written down, and tends to take place face to face. In the early and mid twentieth century several collections of letters on spiritual direction were published where the director and recipient communicated mainly if not entirely through letter. In such correspondence we can find frank, deeply personal and insightful commentaries on the steps and stages of the spiritual journey that, though written in the particular style of the time, can also help our contemporary understanding. Evelyn Underhill writes to one correspondent:

> The light comes, when it does come, rather suddenly and strangely I think. It is just like falling in love; a thing that never happens to those who are always trying to do it.
>
> You may also take it for granted, of course, that so long as you want peace and illumination for your own sake you will not get them. Self-surrender an entire willingness to live in the dark, in pain, anything – this is the real secret. I think no one really finds the Great Companion till their love is of that kind that they long only to give and not to get.[2]

As the third step of love deepens, so the implications of what has been done *to* us in our relationship with God emerges through our lives, and in our spiritual practice. In other words, we experience the third step of love, rather than bringing it into being through thinking about it or categorising it. Perhaps our self-consciousness decreases, so that although we recognise that we are being continuously converted, we are less consciously observing ourselves and more bound up in the actual process.

The changes can, at times, and for some, feel healing and liberating. For example, Rufus Jones, the Quaker, writes about the gradual dawning upon him:

> A 'restoration' of another sort had gone on. I seemed in a new way to be liberated from fears and anxieties and

worries. I had entered into an unsuspected tranquillity and peace ... spiritual energies of a more or less permanent order flowed in and operated as though God at my fountains far off had been raining.[3]

For others who write about their experiences, the deepening of the third step becomes at times an increasingly uncomfortable place. Loving God for himself seems anything other than a tepid sentimentality or a cosy mindset where all is light and joy. Friedrich von Hügel describes Christianity as heroism – it's nothing about being nice, or not being bad tempered – it's not wishy-washy. Rather, 'Christianity is an immense warning; a tremendous heroism.'[4] Perhaps what is being described here is the strength of the inner, and sometimes outer, struggle that takes place. If we love God for himself our relationship with him involves the acknowledgement of uncertainty. Who is this God that we love? What does 'loving him for who he is – for "himself"' mean? We are taking on what is inexplicable to our rational minds. Therefore, if God is something more than we can explain and understand then our relationship implies our own littleness. It has to involve a giving up and a letting go of who we think we are, or who we appear to be – sometimes described as a process of stripping. It also has to involve a letting go of where we think we should be, or how we think we should be serving God, or our conception and definition of being a Christian. As we deepen our understanding of this third step of love so we move further away from the first step of love and from our self-love and self-preoccupation.

There's a good example of this when Thomas Merton, who has been planning his entry into a Franciscan monastery, has a sudden moment of realisation of the implications of being in relationship with God: 'I had fallen asleep in my sweet security. I was living as if God only existed to do me temporal favours.' This begins a process of new understanding about his potential vocation. He writes: 'It is only when we have lost all love of our selves for our own sakes that our past sins cease to give us any cause for suffering or for the anguish of shame.'[5] Part of deepening our intimacy with God is accepting what happens to us as God's plan, even when it goes against our own ideas and desires. The phrase 'relationship' with God does involve mutuality and clearly a connection with him, but not in the sense we understand it with one another. This has to be another order of relationship altogether. Our relationship with God involves a sense of deep exposure, with the associated suffering and sacrifice, and ongoing conflict and questioning. This process of stripping can happen as part of the Christian journey in a voluntary sense – we can believe that this is what we want to aim for – or it happens eventually anyway through distress, illness and death. The stripping eventually pares us down to the essential – which, as Paul Tillich describes it, is our ultimate concern and the ground of our being, which is God.

Relocation of the centre of gravity

Events happen, and as we are guided and taken to new experiences, so inevitably part of the third step of love is recognising the otherness of God, and the impossibility of limiting any experience of God by language. Sometimes, instead, we are left with images imprisoned in terms that barely touch on what has happened as our life is being shaped by God's will. Many write about their strange sense of awe, as they begin to appreciate that God's action towards each of us is 'a masterpiece of partiality and love'.[6] We later wonder at the way that the hand of God has led us and opened doors for us. How do we translate such individual and yet universal experiences?

One of Carl Jung's central theories was that the meaning of life was to relocate the centre of gravity of the personality from the ego to the Self. This is another way of saying, in psychological terms, what John the Baptist knew about his relationship with Jesus: 'He must increase, but I must decrease' (John 3:30). For Carl Jung, our centre, which is our source and our ultimate foundation, is the Self – with a capital 'S'. This is different from our individual personal self with a small 's'. Carl Jung wrote about Jesus Christ as the symbol of the Self in a way that has echoes of Paul Tillich's idea of God as the ground of our being and our ultimate concern. For Carl Jung the Self is the place of transcendence of both the conscious and unconscious: 'Christ is himself God, an all-embracing totality ... self-realization – to put it in religious or metaphysical terms – amounts to God's incarnation.' This third step of love burdens us, according to Carl Jung, with the fate of losing ourselves in a greater dimension and being robbed of our fancied freedom of will.[7]

In loving God for what he is, and together with the beginnings of our comprehension of what Jesus has done to us, we become increasingly conscious of our separation from God. Eckhart Tolle reminds us that the Greek root of the word 'sin' offers us an understanding that sin means to miss the target.[8] In other words, we sin when we miss the point of our existence, which is to love and be with God. As we move deeper into the vertical dimension of our relationship with God so we recognise our distance and therefore we see our sin. Yet to see, hear and know the splendour of God we do need to stand apart from him, and see ourselves in this relationship with him. In this very process of the third step of love we can see ourselves in a new light, and it may be that at this point we can start to see the illusory nature of the self with a small 's' that we have constructed.

Robert Johnson sees that in our separation from what we

are observing lies the alienation of a human life. The sense of being separated lies with the ego. For while we need the egoic structure to function in the world, the framework gives us a separate sense of 'I' and that is precisely the distance from all else that makes us feel so lonely. 'One must then find a way to restore the unity with God, to worship … We must separate from God before we can reunite with God.'[9]

Realising what has been done to us makes us accountable to God

If God begins to become the master of our internal house then we move to being accountable to him. He may be as a servant in that position, helping and guiding us, but as our love deepens, so does our dependence and need of this servant/master. In Etty Hillesum's writings she tracks this movement in her relationship with God. The internal movements of stripping and exposure are mirrored by her external situation. She writes of the tightening restrictions on her physical life and needs as the Nazi persecution of the Jewish people in the Netherlands increases. Etty Hillesum says that in describing the growing intimacy of her relationship with God she is more bashful than if she were writing about her love life. As she monitors her inner feelings and places these against the events in the external world, she notes that as the emphasis shifts increasingly towards the inner life, so she becomes less and less dependent on external circumstances. Perhaps, too, when her circumstances change, she thinks that now there is something 'tough and indestructible' inside her that will help her, 'never give up, never escape, take everything in, and perhaps suffer; that's not too awful either, but never, never give up'.

In the transformation that is taking place within her, Etty Hillesum seems able to hold the pain and the suffering in mind without flinching from the reality of what is happening. In that understanding she feels fear, but can also regain some inner peace as she realises that she is accountable only to God: 'I don't think life is meaningless. And God is not accountable to us for the senseless harm we cause one another. We are accountable to Him.' She writes that her life has become extended by death: 'Every day we shed more trivia', concentrating on the essentials – the stripping of the illusions of life are happening both materially and spiritually and very fast. In the process Etty Hillesum feels connected with eternity, and with 'millions of others from many centuries, and it is all part of life'. 'There is no need to put on a show, I have my inner strength and that is enough, the rest doesn't matter ... And a contentment that rests in God' and acceptance of everything. She holds to a belief that even as we die 'a terrible death we are able to feel right up to the very last moment that life has meaning and beauty, that we have realised our potential and lived a good life. I can't really put it into words.'[10]

The stripping process – *ascesis* as it is sometimes called – the letting go of our will and our surrender to the will of God deepens our love for God. We are able to love God for himself. There is no competition, the path is becoming clear, and so to repeat the gospel guidance: 'He must increase, but I must decrease' (John 3:30). In the third step of love, it is as if our very being is in a process of becoming, as it is honed down and clarified in the light. In our answer to Jesus' question we begin to understand that this is what is happening to each of us.

Practical suggestions linked to the third step of love and the third question

Exercise 1: Where is God in my life?

Take your 100-word life story and from this draw a time line, beginning with birth and marking where you are now. Mark the main external events above the line and the psychological issues below the line. Draw a similar line with spiritual changes and practices marked on them. See if there are any connections or patterns.

Exercise 2: Intimacy audit

Thinking about our response to these statements is a way of reflecting upon our closeness to God:

- In the last 24 hours I felt closest to God when …
- In the last 24 hours I felt furthest from God when …

The time can be changed to within an hour or expanded to think about the last week or even month.

If we are trying to be honest with God we can also think about the following statements and see if there is any correlation with our intimacy with God:

- In the last 24 hours I felt most true to my self when …
- In the last 24 hours I felt at my most false when …

Look over the intimacy audit and at your life time line. Is there a particular personal quality that may act as an obstruction to deeper intimacy? We often obscure our relationship with God through pride or self-criticism, guilt or fear, or feelings of inadequacy. Explore and describe this quality and see if by bringing it into consciousness it's possible to reduce the power and control.

86

Sometimes we can monitor situations where this might be especially strong. Bring the quality that acts as an obstruction into the presence of Jesus and through prayer ask for his help with healing. Ask that with his love and compassion the obstruction within can melt away.

Suggestions

Keeping a spiritual journal

A spiritual journal can be a place both to note down events in our inner world and our outer world that link to our spiritual journeying. We might include our dreams and thoughts about them, recognition of our projections, consolations and revelations with a small 'r', as well as reflections on passages from the Bible, encounters with people, books, films, poems and songs that have meant something to us.

In our jottings we can look for clues sent by God that may point us in our next step, or signs of the manifestation of God in our life. Always we can ask of things that happen to us: why is this happening now and what does it mean spiritually? As this is private we can also be uncritically creative in what we write. We can see if the quality of our relationship with God is deepening.

Learning spiritual songs or hymns

Learning by heart songs, hymns, psalms or parts of the liturgy or Bible is also one way of keeping our minds centred on God. Sometimes the tune or the words can help us in times of distress or emptiness, or when we are bored or distracted. Rosemary Hartill describes learning by heart Psalm 100 at school and wishing she'd been taught more: 'I have met Ugandans and Chinese who told me that reciting psalms by memory was the way they'd psychologically survived imprisonment, torture and persecution.'[11]

Self-analysis of the scattered self, spiritual direction and going on retreat

Here are three suggestions for beginning to understand what Jesus has done and is doing within us. The first is self-analysis, which is something we can do on our own.

When we try to pray, meditate and contemplate, our mind can often become distracted. Letting go of what comes to mind (the analogy with passing clouds) is usually recommended, but sometimes if the distraction keeps happening and it becomes increasingly difficult to dismiss, it can help to analyse what it is that is distracting us. From this we can build a picture of what can be described as the scattered self. From our analysis of the distractive thoughts we might find the following:

- It may be thoughts about what we feel we ought to be doing apart from sitting in prayer. This we can analyse as diversion.
- It may be thoughts about events that have recently disturbed us – perhaps something we or someone else has said or done. We can sift through this and see whether there is some aspect that we need to work further on, or that we need to bring briefly into our prayer space and then let go of.
- It may be something from long ago, some forgotten incident or earlier emotion. This may need more attention. This could be something to write down and to return to later, away from the prayer space.

The idea of spiritual direction offers us support and guidance on our steps towards God. Spiritual direction is one way in which we can be steered in our faith and in our ongoing relationship with God. It can help us in our not knowing and our uncertainty. Finding someone with whom we can discuss our religious life and our spiritual practices is an important part of deepening our relationship with God.

Having a few days on retreat is a chance to deepen seriously our love of God. We are free to spend time alone with God.

There are led retreats and retreats that offer a place and space. Some retreat houses offer spiritual direction and individual guided retreats. Both spiritual direction and going on retreat gives us encouragement and help. It can also give us a sense of community and another place where we can feel at home.

Prayers

1.   O God I seek to know you in prayer
    to have the joy of knowing that you are.
    I know that I cannot
        objectify you
        describe you,
        reduce you to propositions,
        but only understand by faith.
    Reveal yourself to me, I pray, through the records
    of Jesus Christ and through his everlasting presence
        with me.[12]

2. A prayer by Thomas à Kempis for the end of the day that the will of God may be fulfilled:

> O most merciful Jesus, grant to me your grace that it may be with me, and labour with me and persevere with me even to the end. Grant that I may always desire and will that which to you is most acceptable and dear. Let your will be mine, and let my will ever respond to yours in perfect accordance. Let me desire what you desire and hate what you hate, and let me desire and hate nothing but what you desire and hate. Let me die to all that is of this world and for your sake rejoice to be despised and ignored in this generation. Grant me, above all other desires, the desire to rest in you, that my heart may find its peace in you. You are the peace of the heart, you are its only resting place, apart from you all things are harsh and restless. In this peace, in

this very peace which is yourself, the one supreme and eternal good, I will sleep and rest. Amen.[13]

Thought: love of God from Abbé de Tourville

Spend your time in loving our Lord as simply as possible and without any afterthought, just because He is the ideal and He belongs to you. He is so gentle and humble of heart that it is pure delight to talk to Him quite frankly, without any spiritual tension, in complete simplicity ...

Love our Lord tranquilly in the knowledge that He is infinitely loveable; that is all. After that it is for Him to take charge of us, and He will not be found wanting.[14]

CHAPTER TEN

From the third step of love
to the fourth

This chapter explores the place of humility in self-surrender, and also the idea of the connections between the material and spiritual dimensions – both aspects of the space between the third and fourth steps of love.

Humility

In the early sixth century one of the central commitments of the Rule of St Benedict was to humility. St Benedict uses the words that Jesus repeated on two occasions: 'For all who exalt themselves will be humbled, and those who humble themselves will be exalted' (Luke 14:11; 18:14). Humility is about finding our right relationships in life, and as part of the whole of creation. Benedict directs us to know our place in the universe, our connectedness, our dependence on God and our corresponding littleness, and uses the symbolism of Jacob's ladder to explain the twelve steps of humility as part of the monastic vocation. Six centuries later St Bernard wrote, in the Benedictine tradition, *On the degrees of humility,* and in this he took St Benedict's degrees and looked at the dangers of pride as the other side of humility. Thomas Merton writes that the strength of St Bernard lay in his humility, and this made it impossible for him to place any confidence in his own weakness, and that 'drove him in turn to an unlimited confidence in our Divine Redeemer and His most Blessed Mother'.[1] Humility would seem to be an inevitable part of the process of letting go of self-will and turning to God.

The root of the word comes from the word *humus* meaning soil, and so in humility we accept that we come from and will return to dust, and also that the very ground of our being is our dependence on God. Humility is part of the bedrock of spiritual life. Unfortunately the contemporary connotations of the word are negative and rather unhealthy – if we humiliate ourselves it is seen as a blow to our self-esteem and well-being. So being humble does not seem to be a twenty-first-century attribute, but in the religious context it is linked to the move away from self-centredness. If we are increasingly orientated to God then we are less interested in ourselves, and understand better all our limitations. When we realise what we are looking for, who Jesus Christ is for us, and what he has done to us, then we see we are only complete with him.

Mary

Mary's humility, obedience and surrender characterise this transitional space between the third and the fourth step of love. In her response to God we see her surrender control: 'Here am I, the servant of the LORD; let it be with me according to your word' (Luke 1:38). Far from being an act of masochistic submission this becomes an affirmation of life and freedom. The Magnificat (Luke 1:46–55) could even serve as an anthem for both the third step of love, as it is full of Mary's sense of God's mysterious and life-affirming actions, and also for the necessary humility and self-surrender leading to the fourth step.

Mary is central to St Bernard's teachings and experience of Christian spirituality. His focus is on the freedom of Mary's consent as the supreme example of action, and her receptivity to the indwelling of the Word as a model of contemplation – this represents the harmonious balance between these two aspects of the life of faith. St Bernard writes that Mary's longing for 'the incarnation of the Word is cause as well as model for Christians' hunger and thirst for union with Christ'.[2] This is made possible only through Mary's total surrender to God's will. In her reply she reduces everything to the 'complete and utter abandonment of the soul to God's will under whatever form it was manifested'.[3]

What does it mean to surrender in this way to God's will? Why and how does it happen? Is it really up to us, or is it something that happens *to* us? Answers to these questions are only intimated in the gospel accounts of Mary's earthly life. For de Caussade she is the embodiment of mystical theology and models for us the faithful co-operation of the soul with the work of God. In his view we do not need to understand any of this, but only to submit to it – this can happen if we let go of our own desires. For God's action to be embodied within us means 'recognizing the designs of God for us at the present moment'.[4] Humility means that we lay open who we think we are, and what we think we do, to God's transformational action. We let go of the fantasy of our omnipotence, which needs humility.

De Caussade's emphasis on being in the present moment and realising the fullness of God within the present moment is echoed by the contemporary spiritual teachings of Eckhart Tolle. He speaks and writes about 'the power of now' and 'the surrender to what is'. If we can interrupt our incessant self-centred thinking, and move to a place of thoughtlessness (i.e. no-thought) awareness, then we are connected to pure consciousness which is the kingdom of God. Eckhart Tolle explains that true surrender does not mean passively putting up with things, but is rather the 'profound wisdom of *yielding* to rather than *opposing* the flow of life'. It means accepting the present moment unconditionally and without reservation, 'it is to relinquish inner resistance to what *is*' and 'to accept the "isness" of this moment'.[5] This does not mean we take no action, but that the responses we make are not weighed down by emotional negativity or judgement. In other words we develop our conscious awareness.

Surrender

Perhaps it makes more sense now to return to the route described by Brother Lawrence, the seventeenth-century French monk referred to earlier. He suggests the practice of fixing ourselves in the presence of God by 'conversing all the time with him', and referring all actions to him. Although he warns that this initially takes some perseverance, he says we need to act very simply with God, asking him for help in each and every situation as it arises. He writes about submission to God's will through keeping 'the soul's gaze on God'. This can take different forms, such as: a remembering of God; an alertness towards God; a hazy vision of him; a wordless conversation, and throughout maintaining a deep confidence in God as the life and peace of the soul. All our actions are a chance for fellowship with God.[6] Brother Lawrence suggests that we should regularly interrupt everything we do, and even if only for a few moments pause 'to worship God in the depths of our heart, to savour him, though it be but in passing, and as it were by stealth'. We need to hold to our faith and belief that God is in our hearts, and turn to him with all our conflicts and shortcomings.[7]

Several centuries later, Raissa Maritain describes the separation from self-will as a calming of her soul and as a detachment:

> What joy to break oneself and to give something to Him who gives us all! ... I seem to feel my soul detached, freer, as if a bond had been broken. I imagine a kernel which has been turned round and round inside the pulp of the fruit, if that were possible, so as to make it lose its adhesions.

She writes of a separation within her, as if there are two aspects to what is happening to her: events and associated emotions and experiences in the foreground, with the background fixed in faith and love in God. Over time what was previously to the fore retreats to the background, while the background becomes the centre of her life. Raissa is writing of the developing process of her abandonment to God:

> The mind and will thoroughly given to God, thoroughly fixed in him – the heart, the sensibilities can still experience various passions, and offer so to speak, the matter of an independent life but not the form, since the will does not consent.

The sacrifice of self-will and the stripping process involve what she describes as partial deaths. For her it is a testimony of her faith, and also part of her homage to God. Yet she describes the painful nature of this stripping process: 'I suffer so much, in spite of appearances ... Today everything is suffering and lives by suffering, there is no earthly refuge.'[8]

We sacrifice our self-will by laying it aside. We take our emotional, intellectual and moral selves out of the present situation, whether it is good or bad. This means that we still can observe how events are and the human emotions we are subject to, but there is another part of us, which is our inner attention, which remains fixed on God. In this way some essential part of us becomes dedicated to God and separated out from the persona and self we have constructed. It is at this point that our awareness of what we might call the false illusory self and our true self, the self we are meant to be, becomes even clearer.

The space between step three and step four of love requires humility in order to relinquish the illusory self. We take it 'out of common use and ... make it over to God'. Bede Griffiths describes how the inward offering has to take place in the very centre of our being, where we alone encounter God who is hidden in the depths of every soul. He writes how he had been led to break with the material world and to control his natural desires and renounce his own reason – to surrender the very centre of himself. Bede Griffiths experiences this as love, but a love with a terrifying power that demanded everything, and which was a torment if it was resisted. He writes that once the surrender had been made this became a force that took over the direction of his life:

> I had been striving to come to terms with it, to allot it a certain place in my life but it had shown me that it would accept no compromise. I had wanted to keep my own will and to direct my own life; but now I had been forced to surrender. I had placed my life in the hands of a power which was infinitely beyond me and I knew from this time that the sole purpose of my life must be to leave myself in those hands and to allow my soul to be governed by that will.

To live with humility and to surrender to this power which is both within us and yet so much more than our self takes us beyond reason, and away from our usual conceptions and rationalisations. Adrift in this new territory we are helped by Christ. 'The sacrifice of Christ is the central event in human history; it is the event which alone gives meaning to life.' Attempting to follow the example of Mary, and of many who have taken these steps before us, our continuous conversion to Christ is about submitting to a process of death and resurrection in ourselves, 'it is to pass through the world of appearances into the realm of Being'.[9]

Awareness of two dimensions

The four steps of love are about a spiritual journey, a pilgrimage towards a holy place and space. This place of God is a place of mystery. To get there it seems as if we have to let go of the surface world of appearances and things, and, as Bede Griffiths suggests, pass through into another realm which is the realm of true being. Our side of the relationship seems to be to try to keep open, to allow ourselves to become vulnerable and to practise humility, and if we are in relationship with Jesus, then, as Laurence Freeman writes, we are kept 'constantly open to ultimate meaning'.[10] In the space between the third and fourth step of love we may glimpse a further dimension to the life we know. As we come to trust a little more in the spiritual consciousness so we recognise that although objects and things may be as they seem, there is 'a more than' operating within us and beyond us. This is the spiritual dimension beyond the physical and the mental dimension – beyond the psychological categories of the conscious and the unconscious.

What does this really mean? Jesus tells Pilate, 'My kingdom is not from this world' (John 18:36). As we become increasingly involved in our relationship with God we turn from our self and the world of form and things. As Thomas Merton wrote in a letter to Jacques Maritain: 'There are great illusions to be got rid of, and there is a false self that has to be taken off, if it can be done.' He adds, 'There is still much to change before I will really be living in the truth and in nothingness and humility and without any more self-concern.'[11]

Abbé de Tourville writes that we carry a whole world within our souls always.

> It surrounds you and you are impregnated by it. It has become part of you, and since you are its creation and moulded by it, it lives within you. It is God Himself. It is the world of God and of those souls of whom, for various reasons and in varying degrees, you are the true child through the special nature of the grace which has been given to you.[12]

In discovering our spiritual consciousness we realise another dimension to life, we are aware that there is more to life than surface. This is the vertical dimension that Kathleen Raine writes about. The French priest and writer Jean Sulivan brings the vertical dimension into the present moment to make the vertical instant. He notes that in Mark's gospel Jesus is on the move with no permanent dwelling, he is forever crossing over into this land, and over that frontier. Jesus is the nomad, the sojourner travelling alongside the wanderers in the desert. As with so many of those we read about throughout the Bible, we too have to leave where we are settled. As Jean Sulivan says: 'One must create large spaces within oneself, become a passer-by, a foreigner ... it's always a matter of being uprooted. "Be not afraid".' The words that Jesus speaks to us are words that invite us 'to become joyously present in the instant'. Yet we have scarcely begun to uncover the implications of Jesus' words to us. Perhaps we hear them and they sound familiar, but when we really hear them then something different happens. Jesus' four questions to us can lead us on the steps of love towards the homeland which is the place and space of our pilgrimage. Jean Sulivan puts it like this:

So Jesus' word touches you like a hand on your shoulder, a threat as well as a friendship, a fraternal and dangerous invitation that leads from the known world and the deciphered text and makes you cross over to a land that is both here and elsewhere, whose image you carry deep within you.[13]

There is a vertical dimension of spiritual consciousness that is revealed to us as we turn to the mysterious and indescribable God who exists independently from all our projections and conceptions. As we move closer to God, and through his transformational action, some of what is spiritual unconsciousness is brought into consciousness. We struggle to describe spiritual experiences and the realisation that there is another reality than the one we know. We can define this as two dimensions, or two worlds. There is the outer world and the inner, there is earth and heaven. Jesus describes to Nicodemus that there is a physical birth into the world and a new birth or rebirth into spiritual life: 'Very truly, I tell you, no one can see the kingdom of God without being born from above.' And again in answer to Nicodemus' question: 'Very truly, I tell you, no one can enter the kingdom of God without being born of water and Spirit. What is born of the flesh is flesh, and what is born of the Spirit is spirit.' Sometimes, as with Nicodemus, this is too difficult for us. Jesus' response again highlights the two dimensions: 'If I have told you about earthly things and you do not believe, how can you believe if I tell you about heavenly things?' (John 3:3–12).

Many spiritual teachers and writers seem to have some understanding of these two dimensions although they use different words to describe them; some live as if with one foot in each dimension or each world – an increasingly transitional space. It is then that the feeling of being a stranger and a sojourner on earth becomes stronger. One way is to think of the created, which is everything in the world, and the uncreated, which some describe as the creator. Johannes Jorgensen uses the words natural and supernatural to distinguish the material from that which offered a glimpse of something transcendent.

Etty Hillesum picks up the same distinction in holding to a spiritual reality that was beyond the natural suffering of which she was also a part. When Carl Jung struggles to explain the difference between the ego and the self, and the Self with a capital 'S', he is speaking of this same realisation. Thomas Merton uses the idea of the false and true self to explain his experiences. Robert Johnson describes it as the ordinary world and the Golden World. Raissa Maritain writes of the human and inhuman, and the space of the passion of Christ where the two meet. Dom John Chapman writes about the changing and the changeless – the time limited and the outside of time. He urges those to whom he wrote to separate their feelings from their will. If the will is focused on God nothing else matters. In time the feelings come and go and are less important because of their transitory nature, but our will can be linked to the dimension which is changeless. Eckhart Tolle talks about the same idea when he refers to moving beyond the world of form. He describes this as stepping back from the polarity of things, from the world of objects (and he includes thoughts as part of the world of object consciousness), into space consciousness.[14] Kate Turkington, in her exploration on cross-cultural spiritual experiences, writes of her 'Everlasting moment' where she experiences the other dimension: 'I sit frozen in time and space, all-seeing, all-knowing, very wise … I am engulfed in a feeling of perfect love.' Great peace descended on her and she acknowledges, 'Yes, there is a Peace that passeth all understanding and this is it.' As someone who begins her search as a cynic and non-believer she is left with the experience, 'I am in touch with the divine.'[15]

The idea of the two dimensions is implicit in many of the psalms, including:

> How lovely is your dwelling-place, O LORD of hosts!
> My soul longs, indeed it faints for the courts of the LORD;
> Happy are those who live in your house …
> For a day in your courts is better than a thousand else-
>   where. (Psalm 84:1–2, 4, 10)

Connections

Clearly the two dimensions are connected and not actually separate realms at all. As we turn increasingly towards God, then something from the unmanifested flows into our manifest world, and as we know, makes it and us more benevolent. As we become the channel then the polarities become less acute. One way in which we understand this is when we use the idea of God as love. Love flows from the other dimension into the world of form, into creation. The person of Jesus Christ embodies this experience and this connection between the dimensions. This is the incarnation. The cross marks the central point of the intersection of the vertical dimension with the horizontal – the surface level. As we develop in our relationship with Jesus, so we are opening ourselves to the love that comes from one dimen-sion into the manifest world. We are becoming the human self we are meant to be. We are changed, from our creation in the world in the image of God, into the likeness of Christ. The four steps of love are the movement towards that realisation. In one sense they are then the journey to the place of the cross and of Jesus' crucifixion.

Some spiritual writers find that the essence of their being lies in the other realm, but that their union with Christ's humanity deeply alters how they are in this world – as the illusions of the manifest world, and our part in it, are stripped away, so we feel increasingly drawn to genuinely loving God and others. The four steps of love gradually move us from both feet in one world, to one foot in each world, and finally at our death to both feet in the other world. As Laurence Freeman writes, the 'difference between the beginning and the end of the journey is simply that we are fully conscious at the end'.[16]

CHAPTER ELEVEN

>‹‹

The fourth step of love:
'We love ourselves for God's sake'

Sт Bernard's four steps of love are based on the idea that love is our whole reason for existing, and that the development that takes place in our spiritual life is almost like a process of re-education that gradually moves us away from self-love towards loving God and that of God in the other people that we meet. In the fulfilment of the final step we love ourselves for God's sake. In other words, we no longer love our self except with God, through God and for God. We finally understand that in God we live and move and have our being, and that ultimately our true self is in him. St Bernard, and those who have commented later on his text, understand that in this life this fourth degree of love may rarely be attained, and then only for a short time.

> I would say that person is blessed and holy to whom it is given to experience something of this sort, so rare in life, even if it be but once and for the space of a moment. To lose yourself, as if you no longer existed, to cease completely to experience yourself, to reduce yourself to nothing, is not a human sentiment but a divine experience.

Therefore the fourth step cannot be fully arrived at until death, and certainly cannot be achieved through our own attempts. It will be something that happens to us – an act of grace. St Bernard writes that it will happen to us when we are no longer constrained by our physicality. It is when we move fully out of the material dimension and into the spiritual dimension.

> Hence it is in a spiritual and immortal body, calm and pleasant, subject to the spirit in everything, that the soul hopes to attain the fourth step of love, or rather to be possessed by it … it is not obtained by human efforts. I mean we will easily reach the highest step of love when we will no longer be held back by any desire of the flesh nor upset by troubles, as we hasten with the greatest speed and desire toward the joy of the Lord.

For St Bernard losing the self in the fulfilment of the fourth step of love is a divine experience. It is the culmination of our longing and hunger for God, and the place where the words of the Lord's Prayer, 'Thy will be done on earth as it is in heaven', are fulfilled. He likens the experience to the drop of water disappearing in wine; to molten iron taking the form of fire; and to the air transformed into sunshine on a sunny day: 'so it is necessary for the saints that all human feelings melt in a mysterious way and flow into the will of God.' Otherwise, he adds, 'how will God be all in all if something human survives in us?'[1]

Contemporary understanding of the fourth step

Psychologically we need to love ourselves, and obviously while we are alive our biological instinct to survive ensures that we naturally put ourselves before God. This means that it is not possible to attain fully to the fourth step of love where 'we love ourselves for God's sake', while we are still bound by our physical bodies. However, the continuous conversion that takes place gradually in us through journeying along the path means that we can sometimes have a glimpse of the fourth step of love. In this chapter we explore this glimpse both as a foretaste and a foreseeing; we can 'taste and see' and 'come and see' what it might be like to lose ourselves in our love for God.

How can we imagine this fourth step of love? There are times when we are forced to relinquish all that we are for a vertical instant and can anticipate what it is like to love ourselves for God's sake. In other words, what we realise in that moment is that our orientation has completely altered. Our eyes have been opened so that we no longer look towards ourselves, rather we look towards God, and in seriously looking at God we also begin to see ourselves as we seriously and truly are.

If we understand the four steps of love, which Etienne Gilson calls 'the apprenticeship of charity', as a path of continuous conversion and gradual assimilation with the divine life, then it makes sense that this last step can only be glimpsed in this life. It can happen in our action towards another; we can experience it in moments of suffering, and it can sometimes be captured in poetry; and it may happen in contemplation as explored in the next chapter. However, as the fourth step of love can only be fully known as we make the transition through death, Gilson, commenting on the text, writes that to move into the fourth step of love where we rise to pure love of God is to pass out of this life, and

> to live already the life of the blessed in heaven … never in any state is human love for God in this life an absolutely pure love – and that is why there will always be a clearly defined breach between even the most sublime of mystic states and the beatific vision.[2]

Conversion to really being ourselves

Thomas Merton, writing about this state of being, understands the fourth step as the high point of St Bernard's

Christian humanism, as ultimately it means that we are not lost in God, rather, in our true self, we can be found in God in all our personal and individual reality. In other words, taking on the likeness of Christ we become more ourselves as God's will is done in us, 'tasting our eternal happiness ... in the fact that we see His will is done in us'.[3]

The process of letting go of self involves the letting go of fear and desire, the two propelling drives that characterise our lives. If these are transfigured through the Christian experience then the soul is set free to pass beyond them. The characteristic of the fourth step of love is the emptying of our self which we have constructed, and which we use to find our place in the world. We move beyond our self in our absorption with God. In the space that is left in that deepest part of our being we find our lost likeness to Christ. Recognising himself in us, God is reunited with himself, or, in the language of the medieval theologians, the soul – our soul has become Christ's betrothed and united with him. It is the end point and the ultimate conversion.

Those who have journeyed here suggest that as we discover our true self, we feel our reality and our aliveness in our being. As we move from being 'just' an image of God to becoming 'a likeness' with Christ so our inner conflicts gradually end. Etienne Gilson puts it like this: 'When a divine likeness, thus restored, knows herself again in herself, she recognises in herself the God whose likeness she bears. Seeing herself, she sees Him.'[4]

A foretaste of the fourth step through the sacrament of suffering

For some of us it can be hard to sustain our love for God while we, or those whom we love, are in pain and suffering. Suffering takes us into the dark of the night where no morning light seems apparent. The love that we have expressed in the second and third steps of love for what God gives us, and for him, can be seriously tested under such stress. Can we really love God if there seems no advantage in our doing so? Can we genuinely keep the faith and trust in his love? Suffering can certainly wake us up. It can also strip away our normal, everyday self and way of living. It can pare us down to the essentials and can either separate us or bring us closer to God.

There are many accounts of the transformative moments experienced in suffering. Walter Martin, a seriously ill Quaker, wrote about his developing awareness of the supremacy of the spirit over the body. Although he admits his struggle to attain this, he feels that his 'real self, namely the spiritual, has been considerably enhanced ... it is simply the start of a new life'.[5] The way of suffering can also be understood by some Christians as a sacrament and the way of the passion. It is not a glorification of pain, but rather to do with recognition and compassion. Those who go there tell us that it can bring us into identification with Jesus and his passion. The pain and suffering we carry in our bodies can be seen as a form of service in our love for God, a God who also suffers. In this we are one with and feel compassion for all those millions who suffer. Finding a foretaste of the fourth step of love through pain involves becoming even closer to the suffering God. Rather than resisting the pain it can be accepted: 'Acceptance deprives icy meaninglessness of its power because it clings to God's warmth also in suffering.'[6]

We find one of the most moving accounts of the potentially transformative power of acceptance of suffering in the late letters sent by Etty Hillesum from the concentration camp at Westerbork: 'Accepting your own doom needs inner strength.' Commenting on the statement 'And yet God is love', she writes to a friend, 'I completely agree, and it is truer now than ever.' She describes her state of mind as one of 'mournful contentment', and writes that the inner realms of spirit and soul remain spacious and unending even among physical and mental suffering and the threat of imminent death. She uses the metaphor of the spider that casts its main threads before itself and then follows from behind. 'The main path of my life stretches like a long journey before me and already reaches into another world.' She writes of her life as an uninterrupted dialogue with God, 'one great dialogue'.

> Sometimes when I stand in some corner of the camp, my feet planted on Your earth, my eyes raised towards Your heaven, tears sometimes run down my face, tears of deep emotion and gratitude. At night, too, when I lie in my bed and rest in You, O God, tears of gratitude run down my face, and that is my prayer ... I just end up with one single word: God. And that says everything.[7]

Both Dietrich Bonhoeffer and Simone Weil chose 'agony' – an act of compassion by entering into the pain of others – over 'numbness' or apathy – the not wanting to know about suffering. Dietrich Bonhoeffer writes that the way of Christian discipleship can lead from the initial actions of wanting God's help ('pleading for help, praying for fortune and bread' – the 'religion of those not come of age'), to 'being dragged into the messianic suffering of God in Jesus Christ' in which human beings share God's impotence. 'This is the very reversal of everything the religious person expects from God ... to share in God's suffering, to suffer with God the godlessness of the world.'[8] Participation in the sacrament of suffering, which is clearly not at all the same as the self-love and self-importance of personal masochism, can lead us closer to God. It can bring us to a place where we forget ourselves in compassion.

Expression of the fourth step through poetry

It is often in poetry or fragments of prose that we can find the experiences of others who describe a glimpse of the fourth step of love. It may also be the way in which we too try to frame what is happening to us in the darkness of suffering or the light of Christ's presence. The words can only ever be an approximation but can still connect to us. Perhaps this links to the spare use of words, each one containing the weight of much reflection and care.

In Jacques Maritain's preface to Raissa's journal, he writes that in a sense she has said everything in her poetry: 'Were they not born there where, in the strange way things flow together, all sources join within the soul, and where the creative experience of the poet is only the pure mirror of his spiritual experience.'[9] In her poetry, everything is pared down to a reflective simplicity. Raissa Maritain writes of the encounter with Poetry (she gives the word a capital letter as she did with Truth and the Absolute when she meant it as a divine gift and the one, the highest, the essence), in the innermost core of life, of thought and of consciousness. For her the poetic creation emerges from 'absorption into a silence stripped to the uttermost of forms and words', an inner withdrawal from the senses. It is the fruit of the contemplative experience and a glimpse of the fourth step of love, 'God. Poetry. An absolute straight and pure inner activity goes to the one and to the other – goes, sometimes, *from* the one *to* the other.'[10] For her, a saint's life is Poetry. She writes:

> All is Light
> All has been given. The anguish is stilled,
>> Death fulfilled.
> How my soul weights light.

My spirit is given to God, in His care,
My heart is pure as mountain air.
Everything is bright.[11]

Ann Griffiths, the eighteenth-century Welsh hymn-writer, was another poet who expressed a foretaste of the fourth step of love, and her deep longing of 'eternal inseparable union and communion with my God'. Her poetry speaks of her gaze, amazement and wonder before God's humanity revealed in the incarnation and the splendour of God. Her awareness is of the overwhelming reality of God and the union with God in Christ. She longs to enter into 'that great world which shall last forever' and where death is the moment of fulfilment and a point of culmination, 'To be able to leave behind every inclination to counter the will of God, all weakness swallowed up by strength, to become fully conformed to the law which is already on one's heart and to enjoy God's likeness forever'. Or, as she puts it in some wonderful lines in one of her hymns, 'I shall pierce through the veil, into the land of infinite astonishment', and in a later verse, 'and the veils, and the imaginings and shrouds have gone, because, my soul stands now, his finished likeness'. As one commentator puts it, 'It is because she already knows it in part that her longing for its fulfilment is so intense.'[12]

The sacrament of service

The basis of the sacrament of service is that every task is done for the glory of God: 'When we give all our mind and strength to the work at hand, we are glorifying God and adding to His creation.'[13] Sometimes we can lose ourselves in compassionate action towards others and gain a glimpse of loving for God's sake. The history of Christianity has many examples of those who by living the faith let go of self to help and serve others.

'I am what I do.' When C. S. Lewis uses this phrase in the context of his conversion he links it to a significant change that took place within him. As he understood it he became free to act without motives. For him the difference implied an authentic integration of who he is with *how* he is.[14] The experience is of immersion in action that is entirely congruent with belief and love for God. It is not action justified with the usual explanations, or done out of self-interest, but is an unselfconscious out-flowing of who we are in our love for God – I really am what I really do. The sacrament of service is then done both in obedience and with humility. We are open to others, and in meeting with them we meet Christ in that person.

> 'For I was hungry and you gave me food, I was thirsty and you gave me something to drink, I was a stranger and you welcomed me, I was naked and you gave me clothing, I was sick and you took care of me, I was in prison and you visited me …
>
> 'Just as you did it to one of the least of these who are members of my family, you did it to me.'
>
> (Matthew 25:35–36, 40)

Simone Weil, who as we saw chose agony rather than apathy, is one example of someone whose actions also led her towards the fourth step of love. Her active participation in a life of denial and involvement in the suffering of others led to her eventual death. She writes of what she calls 'the supernatural virtue of justice' as the most Christian of virtues, and quotes moral virtues from *The Egyptian Book of the Dead*, in

> words as sublime even as those of the Gospel. 'I have never caused anyone to weep. I have never spoken with a haughty voice. I have never made anyone

111

afraid. I have never been deaf to words of justice and truth' … Generosity and compassion are inseparable, and both have their model in God, that is to say, in creation and in the Passion.[15]

The actions we take that bring us closest to God are those that are rooted in the sense that we are all in it together – each of us is part of the body of Christ. Michael Mayne writes of visiting Mother Teresa's Home for the Dying in Calcutta. Between the men's ward, and the beds filled with women and children, there was a small cubicle. He writes that just before he had arrived an old woman had been brought in from the streets in a filthy condition:

> She was barely recognisable as human. 'Come and see', said Sister Luke, and took me across to the curtained-off trough. She drew back the curtain. The trough was filled with a few inches of water, in which was lying the stick-like body of the old woman. Two Missionaries of Charity were gently washing her clean and comforting her at the same time. Above the trough, stuck to the wall, was a simple notice containing four words: 'The body of Christ'.[16]

For some it is through such actions that the kingdom of God is present, and in that moment of deep compassion is a fore-seeing of the fourth step of love. In action the self is emptied, and there is space for the love of God through our love for others.

➤✦

CHAPTER TWELVE

The fourth question:
'For whom are you looking?'

IN THIS FINAL CHAPTER we turn to reflect on the fourth question that Jesus asks us – a question that is completely entwined with the fourth step of love and that is found three times in St John's gospel. The first time is in the context of his arrest when Jesus asks the armed soldiers and police (John 18:4), 'For whom are you looking?' When they answer 'Jesus of Nazareth,' Jesus replies 'I am he.' His directness seems to stun those who are seeking to destroy him, and so Jesus repeats the question. The soldiers repeat the answer, and again Jesus replies 'I am he.' It is in the dark and in a time- and place-limited context when Jesus asks the question for the first two times. In offering himself into the custody of the soldiers to be crucified, he asks for the release of those who are with him – in the darkness Jesus seeks our freedom.

The third time he asks the question is to Mary Magdalene outside the tomb where his body has been laid. It is a question outside of time and place. Initially dark when she reaches the tomb, the dawn is breaking, and Mary, who loves Jesus, is searching for his dead body and crying in deep shock. She believes she has lost everything, her very reason for living. It is at this point of despair and deep suffering, where all is stripped away, that she meets Christ. In John 20:15 we read, 'Woman, why are you weeping? For whom are you looking?' Mary's reply – as with almost all of our replies to Jesus – is almost to miss the point. She doesn't recognise him until he calls her name. As he says her name 'Mary' she knows – and in being known and named by the risen Christ she finds him for herself. She is brought into the dawn light and sees Jesus face to face. He is not now an object and something external to her for her to cling to – 'Do not hold on to me' (John 20:17) – but rather a joyous experience of communion to be integrated in the deepest part of her true self.

Answering Jesus' question in contemplation

The sacrament of contemplation is where we look and can find communion with Christ in the centre of our being, part of the body of Christ and the communion of saints. We are no longer praying in a self-enclosed way fuelled by self-interest, or praying for the results of prayer, for what God gives us. It is prayer based on our serious love of God and (similar to Eastern meditation) is where we bring our loving attention to God. In prayer we present ourselves: 'as a living sacrifice, holy and acceptable to God, which is your spiritual worship … be transformed by the renewing of your minds' (Romans 12:1–2). It is a place of silence and stillness, and a place of no-analysis, no-thought, no self-concern, beyond imagination. Alone and in solitude, we wait for God. We are completely in the present, here and now. This is the space of the vertical instant, a space outside of time. In this place of no-self, we may, like Mary outside the tomb, meet the risen Jesus Christ and yet not recognise him. Laurence Freeman says that contemplation takes us beyond relationship to 'the silent heart of every relation-ship, where the walls dividing us crumble and there we are in union'. As we know our true self, stripped of all that we have constructed, so we are known, 'at the *door* of the true Self, Jesus is known in the Resurrection'. Contemplation then is a deepening of the relationship with God 'in communion ... often described as a *coming home*. Home to ourselves and to our innate capacity for transcendence.'[1]

Thomas Merton writes about contemplation as both a gift from God and also the destiny for which we are created. It is in contemplation that we can know in part the answer to Jesus' question. It is where we know and love God for himself, and where our true self is realised in God. It is where we can anticipate the transformation of our very being in unity with God. Thomas Merton uses the same descriptions for contemplation as he does for death, but insists that there are those who are destined 'to breathe this new atmosphere while they are still on earth'.[2] Both are an entry into 'the hidden ground of love' that is God and the ultimate awakening to the presence of God, the experience of 'pure reality'. It is our fulfilment which is 'grounded in the depths of the personal life of God and the inner dynamic of love'.[3]

Our answer to the fourth question involves acceptance of the death of the self in the presence of the living Christ. For Thomas Merton this is an act – not only of passive submission, but also an active participation in faith and surrender. We accept what we have been, and we return or surrender this being back to the God who made it; in this sacrifice we become free. In conversation with a Buddhist abbot in Bangkok Thomas Merton asks, 'What is "the knowledge of freedom"?' The reply (similar to the journey of the four steps of love) is, you have to ascend all the steps, but then when there are no more steps you must make the leap: 'Knowledge of freedom is the knowledge, the experience, of this leap.' Thomas Merton writes of the recognition that he is somehow, '*on the edge* of great realization'. The realisation of this ultimate reality takes place when he is contemplating the huge Buddha figures at Polonnaruwa in what is now Sri Lanka. Thomas Merton writes that it is as if he is awakened, just for a moment – jerked almost forcibly out of the usual way of thinking, and with an inner clarity. The figures are strange evidence of the awareness – the absolute clearness of what is:

> what matters is clear … everything is emptiness and everything is compassion … I mean, I know and have seen what I was obscurely looking for. I don't know what else remains but I have now seen and pierced through the surface and have got beyond the shadow and the disguise.[4]

Thomas Merton makes the leap, and in his realisation of the ultimate emptiness and compassion of God he answers the fourth question. Here it seems he experiences connection with the projection of his true self, and the connection of that true self with all that is created and uncreated – the human and inhuman; the time limited and the outside of what we call time; the natural and supernatural; the humanity of Jesus Christ and the divinity of God. Here is the moment of transfusion and realisation. It is the moment of true aliveness – finding who we are looking for.

In meeting Christ we meet our true self

If we are given the grace to answer Jesus' question with our very being through a glimpse of the fourth step of love, then inevitably, in the material dimension, this experience can only be transitory, as we obviously need parts of our illusory or false self – our egoic self – to keep us functioning in this world. However, perhaps through our deepening love of God our awareness of the transient nature of the false self and the world of things becomes gradually apparent, so we become in a sense more available – perhaps even more transparent to ourselves and in our relationship with God. 'The veil between the two dimensions is thin here ... meaning the veil which separates earth from heaven ... from the vision of God.'[5] The false self construct becomes thinner, it is easier to let go of, and more often, and we begin to know ourselves and, in the process, God better. Our intention is turned towards God, even if the actualities and externals of life seem to reclaim us repeatedly.

Glimpsing our true self we recognise it as always having been there – the part that we began with, and that began searching for and loving our creator. The self that we construct around it is impermanent, and like a passing shadow. The narrative that is created around our persona, and indeed its very existence, both end when we die. The false self keeps us at the surface of reality in the dimension of things, and so we are dominated by feelings which come and go according to what is happening to us, or whether we are meeting and satisfying our desires. The false self can hide and keeps safe our true self, but in the very protection imprisons us. It can also now be understood as something more banal – almost a comatose state. In his journal Mircea Eliade writes of a story where a banal atmosphere and mediocre characters are gradually transformed. But what came from 'beyond' as well as all the paradisiacal images of the end of the story, were already there from the beginning, 'but camouflaged by the banality of everyday life and, as such, unrecognizable'.[6]

Our truthful answer to Jesus' question is that we are looking not for the time-limited historical Jesus but for the eternal risen Christ that appears to and is within each of us here and now. If that is our answer then our relationship with God is now no longer just an 'add on', or something that can be fitted profitably into our lives – rather it is our whole reason for existing, and until we completely love

God we are not really alive. So how does this full aliveness fit with the idea of the abandonment of the self to the will of God? It is as if on this part of the journey we are living in a state of active anticipation, or conscious awareness, that we have let go of the illusory constructed self; indeed we are projected beyond the self, and are orientated straight towards God who is with us in the present moment. Yet rather than being subsumed or annihilated by this process, it seems instead that in the deepening relationship with God we surrender our false self – there is a sacrificial death in order to free our true self. A death and rebirth needs to happen. This means a continuous dynamic of inner renewal and continuous rebirth. Over time the exterior false self is gradually shed, as Thomas Merton puts it, 'like an old snake skin'. We become gradually our true self which can be defined as the self that God wants us to be. Thomas Merton thought that this inner experience can happen in contemplation, and takes place at the point where dualism breaks down. 'Coming to know God in the divine selfhood and coming to know our true selves converge in a single intuition; our awareness of our total dependence on God.' In crossing the abyss that separates us from ourselves, we become ourselves, and our 'subjectivity is united to the subjectivity of God'.[7] Here is the answer to the fourth question – it lies in the attainment of the fourth step of love. In our true self we live in the likeness of Christ, we love others, and ourselves, in and for God. So perhaps this is also the space where we can really live the commandments that God has given us. '"You shall love the Lord your God with all your heart, and with all your soul, and with all your mind." This is the greatest and first commandment. And a second is like it: "You shall love your neighbour as yourself"' (Matthew 22:37–39).

The truthful answer

In truthfully answering Jesus' fourth question all aspects are altered through God's transformational action, and our orientation is nearly complete. Our centre of gravity is re-located. We may have begun our conversion through the intellect, or emotions, or been drawn through a sense of morality, but as the process approaches completion all is balanced. There is a transformation of heart and mind, there is interior justice, and our new orientation means that we are free to love our neighbour as ourselves because it is clear that we are all one with Christ. St Paul seems to have attained this state of the fourth step of love and answered Jesus' question when he can say, 'It is now not I that live but Christ that lives in me.'

The meeting in the half light of the breaking dawn between Jesus and Mary Magdalene suggests the meeting that will take place within us if we can answer Christ's question in the context of the fourth step of love. The self is still searching in a state of nothingness and death, although it seems that death has stripped the self of even Jesus – the tomb (our cleared mind, our dead body) is empty and there is after all nothing there. Thomas Merton wrote about this point as one of non-being and being – as the 'point vierge':

> The centre of our nothingness where, in apparent despair, one meets God – and is found completely in His mercy …
>
> At the centre of our being is a point of nothingness which is untouched by sin and by illusion, a point of pure truth, a point which belongs entirely to God, which is never at our disposal … This little point of nothingness and of absolute poverty is the pure glory of God in us. It is so to speak His name written in us.[8]

In the crazy violence and darkness of this world the answer

to the question 'For whom are you looking?' is the risen Christ. If we can experience his light, we can look for him through our actions, prayers, sacraments and times of contemplation. In the moment of total surrender – in the half light between night and the dawn we are again looking for him, and his answer to us at this transition is to know us and call us to him. If we search away from the tomb, in other words beyond the immediate physical facts of death, bodies and graves (the place of no-thought), we are once more given the choice, and a new meaning. Jesus Christ asks, 'Why are you weeping? For whom are you looking?' Mary Magdalene is looking in the material dimension for the tangible, the physical and emotional – for time-limited Jesus. In Christ's response there is an incomparable richness which includes the physical, the emotional *and* the spiritual. He knows Mary, and in his absolute knowledge of her she knows both herself and him as the eternal Christ. The relationship does not belong to the old order of relationship, but rather to a different and completely unexpected experience of unity with God. This is a unity that we do not cling to but are absorbed into.

Reaching the point where we are known in our very being we are completely converted. All that was hidden, or repressed, or denied, falls away. All that we built up and relied on for our personal worth, our personal story and our identity is stripped from us. This is it, and here we are looking for our Lord to be with us. We are in the space that is God. Loving God we can now see ourselves as 'who we really are'. This knowing ourselves through our love of God means that our faith has made us whole.

Completion

Our being is changed on the path of the four steps of love in the finding of our true self in God. Then our death is not a negation of our life, but rather complements it. Carl Jung writes that from the point of view of the psyche, 'death is a joyful event, as it is a wedding, "a *mysterium coniunctionis*" as the soul "achieves wholeness" by finding its missing half'.[9] A Quaker, William Littleboy, wrote in 1917 about death as 'the escape of the spirit from its old limitations and its freeing for a larger and more glorious career'.[10] Somewhere between the death of the illusory self and the resurrection of the true self, we are known by name and called into being. The journey to love, described by St Bernard in the four steps, is the journey from self-love to love of God. Our answers to the four questions that Jesus asks us are also the four steps of love and the conversion from the false self to the true self. It is the journey of acceptance of and obedience to the commandments to love that we have been given. The questions that Jesus asks us, and that characterise these four steps of love, first ask us 'what' are we looking for; next, as we grow to understand that we are in relationship with Jesus, the questions ask 'who' he is for us; and, as we begin to love God, 'what' he has done to us; finally, in this fourth question, we are asked for 'whom' we are looking. When Jesus asks 'For whom are you looking?', first in the darkness of death and then in the early morning light of the resurrection, the answer is the divine Self, the point where our true self is united with Christ. This is the point of the cross – the point of the vertical instant. We are taken by Christ into the vertical dimension, into the body of Christ, and he also holds us with his hands nailed on the horizontal level while we still lead our earthly life.

Here, also, is the ultimate realisation: it is not just us who are and have been doing the looking. Christ is searching for us, and each of us is the sheep that is lost and then lovingly found; each of us is the prodigal child who has returned home to a wonderful welcome; each of us is the coin whose retrieval is so joyfully celebrated. Our very being is searched, found and changed: 'LORD you have searched me and known me' (Psalm 139:1). Perhaps then the insight gradually dawns about the nature of the relationship that we are in as we journey along these steps of love. This love is 'the coming towards us of what really and inalterably is, the regard which creates, while faith and hope are the given response from within us to what is; the given response which love calls forth, while we are "on the way"'.[11] It seems as if while on the path of the four steps of love that we have followed, and the four questions that we have been trying to answer, we have been very active, trying hard to do our best, to be open, vulnerable and humble, to let go of our selfishness, to turn to God and to surrender to his will. But, perhaps, after all, as James Alison suggests, like the experiences of the medieval theologians, *we* have been uncovered and discovered and loved, rather than the other way round. It has all been and continues to be something lovingly done and given to us in love.

Practical suggestions linked to the fourth step of love and the fourth question

These exercises and suggestions cannot 'get' us to the fourth step of love but can help us think a little about what a glimpse of it might be like.

Exercise 1:
The fruits of the spirit

There are several parts to this exercise:

- The first is to return to the idea of the circle used after the first step of love. This time draw another circle and inside a smaller circle. Break up the space between the two circles into sections, rather like spokes of a wheel with a central hub, and fill the sections with the different things that make up your life: work (paid or not), family, friends, leisure, God, and any other things that are important. Which of these belongs in the centre? Are we able to put God, or as he appears in Jesus, in the centre of our wheel of life or is something else more important? Think about your response.

- The second part of the exercise is to answer the question: are you creating something lovely for God through your life? Find out by drawing a tree of life. Take the different things that make up your life that you've used above in the circle, and in this part of the exercise write them in the branches of the tree. Let each branch have fruit – large apples – that are the results from or effects of the things that make up your life. What are the fruits of the spirit that you can see from the different parts of your life? Fill in the apples with your answers.

- Finally, think ahead to your deathbed. If you had to give the story of your spiritual life a title what would it be? What would you like to have come to in a spiritual sense when it's time to leave? And what's stopping you here and now from being that spiritually fulfilled person? Reflect with Jesus about your response to these questions.

Exercise 2:
The eternal moment and heavenly poem

Sit or lie in a comfortable position that allows you to relax. Shut your eyes and become aware of your breath – let it be regular and relaxed. Listen to the silence. In the silent space allow the word 'heaven' to float into your mind. Using your imagination, construct a fantasy about being in heaven: where are you – outdoors or inside – and what is it like? Who is with you? What are you doing? What is happening around you? Become aware of sounds, colours and smells. Feel what it is like to be there and enjoy it.

Once you have constructed your heavenly fantasy slowly come back to the present moment and note what feels the saddest part to leave behind? Become aware again of your surroundings. Then find 25 words that describe your fantasy vision and see if you can make a heavenly poem using each word and adding link words where needed so that it makes enough sense.

Suggestions: time for contemplative prayer

Throughout all the steps of love we need to find a space to allow prayer to happen in us rather than just through the words we use. Contemplative prayer is about just being with Jesus who loves us and whom we love – no agenda, no words and thoughts. It is a 'reclining next to Jesus' (John 13:25). It is a physical space, an emotional space and a spiritual space. This is the space for transformation. Can we find this space inside us for prayer on a regular basis? We may be cluttered by activities, physically agitated and mentally fragmented. We have to stop our compulsive activity so as to allow spiritual space within us – but space for what? There has to be space for silence and a space where we look towards Jesus and allow him to look at us. We need to rest, we have to listen, and in our hearts we move to say 'yes'; we answer Jesus in the silence by saying 'yes, this is me here now'. Prayer space is allowing God to act in us through Jesus rather than telling God what we are doing for him, or what we think we know about him. It is an opening up rather than a closing down.

Ruth Burrows writes about 'the ABC of praying: on our side it is a responding and an answering – You look at me, You call me, here I am', but that leads to further questions which are 'Who are You?' and 'What must I do to receive You?'[12]

Here are some different ways of deepening our contemplative prayer life.

Repetitive prayer

If silence is difficult, or we need something written down to hold on to, then it is useful to find a repetitive prayer. In the East there is a long tradition of prayer-wheels and mantras, and in the Roman Catholic Church the rosary functions in the same way.

The finger joints provide an instant way of counting saying a prayer if we do not want to use a rosary. First of all, we need to find a prayer that suits where we are on the journey, and following the pattern of saying the rosary we might begin with the Lord's Prayer and then repeat our own prayer ten times. We can end with the Gloria.

To say this type of prayer we can be anywhere and yet still create a prayerful space for God no matter what else is going on.

Centering prayer

This is a method established by Fr Thomas Keating that uses both silence and a repetitive phrase or single word to bring us back to the silence. The suggestion is for two-syllable words such as Abba, Jesus, Mary, or single words such as peace, love, joy. We can also write out phrases that help us in times of trial and trouble to stay close to God. One that I use is, 'My life is within God.'

John Main suggested as a mantra the ancient Aramaic prayer 'Maranatha, Maranatha', 'Come, Lord. Come, Lord Jesus.'[13]

Prayer

My Lord God, I have no idea where I am going. I do not see the road ahead of me. I cannot know for certain where it will end. Nor do I really know myself, and the fact that I think I am following your will does not mean that I am actually doing so. But I believe that the desire to please you does in fact please you. And I hope I have that desire in all that I am doing. I hope that I will never do anything apart from that desire. And I know that if I do this you will lead me by the right road, though I may know nothing about it. Therefore I will trust you always though I may seem to be lost and in the shadow of death. I will not fear, for you are ever with me, and you will never leave me to face my perils alone.[14]

Thought: meditation from Charles de Foucauld

Now that life is almost at an end for us, the light into which we shall enter at our death begins to shine and to shew us what are realities and what are not. I love this desert, the solitude; it is so quiet and so wholesome; eternal things seem very real and truth invades one's soul. I am very reluctant to leave my solitude and silence for travel. But God's will be done whatever it may be, not only done but preferred, adored, loved and blessed without reserve.[15]

NOTES

Epigraphs

1. Genesis 1:26; Wisdom 2:23b and 2 Corinthians 3:18.
2. Thomas Merton in a letter to Pierre van der Meer in *The School of Charity*, ed. Brother Patrick Hart (San Diego, New York, London: Harcourt Brace Jovanovich Publishers, 1990), p. 139.

Chapter 1 Introducing the four steps

1. Rumi, taken from the preface of Andrew Harvey, *Hidden Journey* (London: Rider, 1991).
2. Abbé de Tourville, *Letters of Direction* (Harrisburg PA: Morehouse Publishing, 2001), p. 72.
3. Peter L. Berger, quoted in V. Bailey Gillespie, *The Dynamics of Religious Conversion* (Birmingham AL: Religious Education Press, 1991), p. 3.

Chapter 2 The idea of continuous conversion

1. St Bernard, *On the Love of God*, trans. Rev. Terence L. Connolly (New York: Spiritual Books, 1937), p. 37.
2. Abbé de Tourville, *Letters of Direction* (Harrisburg PA: Morehouse Publishing, 2001), p. 72.
3. Wilhelm and Marion Pauck, *Paul Tillich: His Life and Thought* (London: Collins, 1977), pp. 1, 2.
4. See Mark Kline Taylor (ed.), *Paul Tillich: Theologian of the Boundaries* (Minneapolis: Fortress Press, 1987). pp. 122–3.
5. Joel Giallanza CSC, 'Three questions for the spiritual journey', *Ministry of Spiritual Direction*, Vol. 38 (1979), pp. 663–7.
6. Gwendolen Greene (ed.), *Letters from Baron Friedrich von Hügel to a Niece* (London: J. M. Dent and Sons Ltd, 1928), p. xv.
7. Michael Ford, *Wounded Prophet* (London: Darton, Longman and

Todd, 1999), pp. 1, 2.

8. M. Basil Pennington OCSO (ed.), *St Bernard of Clairvaux* (Kalamazoo MI: Cistercian Publication, 1977), p. viii.

9. Hymn written by Bessie Porter Head (1850–1936).

10. Sri Aurobindo, *Letters on Yoga* (Pondicherry, 1970), pp. 115–16, quoted in Felicity Edwards, 'Becoming what we know', *Studies of Spirituality*, 13 (2003), pp. 235–62.

11. H. Newton Maloney and Samual Southard (eds), *Handbook of Religious Conversion* (Birmingham AL: Religious Education Press, 1992), p. 95.

12. A. J. Krailsheimer, *Conversion* (London: SCM Press, 1980), p. 1.

13. W. Conn, *Christian Conversion* (New York and Mahwah NJ: Paulist Press, 1986), pp. 172, 194.

Chapter 3 The first step of love: 'We love ourselves for ourselves'

1. St Bernard, *St Bernard of Clairvaux: Selected Spiritual Writings*, ed. M. Basil Pennington (Hyde Park NY: New City Press, 1997), p. 72.

2. Thomas Merton, *The Seven Storey Mountain* (New York: Harcourt, Brace and Co., 1948), p. 200.

3. St Augustine, *Confessions* (London: Penguin Classics, 1961), pp. 60, 85.

4. Dorothee Soelle, *The Silent Cry* (Minneapolis: Fortress Press, 2001), p. 1.

5. Rubem A. Alves, *The Poet, the Warrior, the Prophet* (London: SCM Press, 1990), pp. 76, 86.

6. Alexander Schmemann, *For the Life of the World* (New York: NSCF, 1963), p. 1, quoted by Alves, *The Poet*, p. 77.

Chapter 4 The first question: 'What are you looking for?'

1. St Augustine, *Confessions* (London: Penguin Classics, 1961), p. 111.

2. Christopher Bollas, *Forces of Destiny* (London: Free Association Books, 1989), uses the idea of the 'unthought known' and 'the transformational object' to describe early interactions between mother and baby, from which I have developed the idea of God

as the unthought known and God's transformational action; cf. pp. 10, 213.

3. William Wordsworth, 'Intimations of Immortality from Recollections of Early Childhood' in *Wordsworth: The Penguin Poetry Library* (Harmondsworth: Penguin, 1943), p. 73.

4. J.-B. Pontalis, *Love of Beginnings* (London: Free Association Books, 1993), p. 17.

5. Ernst Bloch in *The Principle of Hope*, quoted Dorothee Soelle, *The Silent Cry* (Minneapolis: Fortress Press, 2001), p. 11.

6. Mircea Eliade, *No Souvenirs Journal 1957–1969* (London and Henley: Routledge and Kegan Paul, 1978), p. 82.

7. Nicholas Berdyaev, *Dream and Reality: An Essay in Autobiography* (London: Geoffrey Bles, 1950), p. 171.

8. Gwendolen Greene (ed.), *Letters from Baron Friedrich von Hügel to a Niece* (London: J. M. Dent and Sons Ltd, 1928), pp. xii, xv.

9. Thomas Merton, *The Seven Storey Mountain* (New York: Harcourt, Brace and Co., 1948), p. 206.

10. Raissa Maritain, *We Have Been Friends Together and Adventures in Grace* (New York: Doubleday, 1961), pp. 40, 67.

11. Maritain, *We Have Been Friends*, pp. 69, 75, 80.

12. Merton, *The Seven Storey Mountain*, pp. 209, 212.

13. Etty Hillesum, *An Interrupted Life: The Diaries and Letters of Etty Hillesum 1941–43* (London: Persephone Books Ltd, 1999), p. 7.

14. Johannes Jorgensen, *Jorgensen: An Autobiography* (New York, London, Toronto: Longmans, Green and Co., 1929), Vol. 1, pp. 34, 76.

15. George Appleton, *The Practice of Prayer* (London and Oxford: Mowbray, 1980), p. 14.

16. Greene (ed.), *Letters*, p. 4.

17. Flavian Burns OCSO, 'Two conferences on monastic prayer', *The Merton Seasonal*, Vol. 31, No. 1 (2006), p. 17.

Chapter 5 From the first step of love to the second

1. *Quaker Faith and Practice: The Book of Christian Discipline of the Yearly Meeting of the Religious Society of Friends* (1994), 1.02 and 1.17.

2. Melvyn Matthews, *Nearer than Breathing* (London: SPCK, 2002), pp. 7, 8.

3. Brother Lawrence, *The Practice of the Presence of God* (London: Hodder and Stoughton, 1981), p. 29.
4. Harry Guntrip, *Personal Relations Therapy*, ed. Jeremy Hazell (Northvale NJ and London: Jason Aronson Inc., 1994), p. 166.
5. Etty Hillesum, *An Interrupted Life: The Diaries and Letters of Etty Hillesum 1941–43* (London: Persephone Books Ltd, 1999), p. 33.
6. Johannes Jorgensen, *Jorgensen: An Autobiography* (New York, London, Toronto: Longmans, Green and Co., 1929), Vol. 1, pp. 179, 191, 194.
7. Margaret Cropper, *Evelyn Underhill* (London: Longmans, Green and Co., 1958), p. 29.
8. V. Bailey Gillespie, *The Dynamics of Religious Conversion* (Birmingham AL: Religious Education Press, 1991), pp. 4–5.
9. Raissa Maritain, *We Have Been Friends Together and Adventures in Grace* (New York: Doubleday, 1961), p. 140.
10. Matthews, *Nearer than Breathing*, pp. 59 and 58.

Chapter 6 The second step of love: 'We love God for what he gives us'

1. Martyn Percy (ed.), *Previous Convictions* (London: SPCK, 2000), p. 16.
2. St Bernard, *St Bernard of Clairvaux: Selected Spiritual Writings*, ed. M. Basil Pennington (Hyde Park NY: New City Press, 1997), p. 74.
3. Abbé Henri de Tourville, *Letters of Direction* (Harrisburg PA: Morehouse Publishing, 2001), p. 84.
4. Kathleen Raine, 'The vertical dimension', *Fairacres Chronicle*, Vol. 31, No. 2 (1998).
5. Pope John XXIII, *Journal of a Soul* (London: Geoffrey Chapman, 1964), p. 76.
6. Johannes Jorgensen, *Jorgensen: An Autobiography* (New York, London, Toronto: Longmans, Green and Co., 1929), Vol. 2, pp. 111–12, 117.
7. Thomas Merton, quoted in William H. Shannon, Christine M. Bochen and Patrick F. O'Connell (eds), *The Thomas Merton Encyclopedia* (Maryknoll NY: Orbis Books, 2002), p. 269.
8. Thomas Merton, *A Search for Solitude* (New York: HarperSanFrancisco, 1996), pp. 150, 181.

9. Christopher Bryant SSJE, *Prayer and Different Types of People*, paper published by SSJE in Oxford, undated, p. 9.

Chapter 7 The second question: 'But who do *you* say that I am?'

1. John Barton and John Muddiman (eds), *The Oxford Bible Commentary* (Oxford University Press, 2001), p. 865.

2. *Quaker Faith and Practice: The Book of Christian Discipline of the Yearly Meeting of the Religious Society of Friends* (1994), 19.02.

3. Laurence Freeman, *Jesus: The Teacher Within* (New York, London: Continuum, 2001), pp. 23, 24.

4. Jeremy Taylor, quoted by Michael Mayne in *A Year Lost and Found* (London: Darton, Longman and Todd, 1987), p. 46.

5. Hymn, 'Will you come and follow me if I but call your name?', written by John Bell and Graham Maule.

6. *The Letters of Evelyn Underhill*, ed. Charles Williams (London: Longmans, Green and Co., 1943), p. 96.

7. Freeman, *Jesus*, p. 61.

8. Thomas Merton, *The Hidden Ground of Love*, ed. William Shannon (London: Collins Flame, 1990), p. 527.

9. Wilfred Bion, *Four Discussions with W. R. Bion* (Perthshire: Clunie Press, 1978), pp. 22, 43.

10. Patrick Kavanagh, 'The great hunger' in *Collected Poems* (London: Brian and O'Keefe, 1972), p. 41, quoted by Kevin O'Gorman, 'In living memory', *Spirituality*, Vol. 12 (2006), p. 38.

11. Dom Aelred Graham, *Zen Catholicism* (New York: Harcourt, Brace and World, 1963), p. 143.

12. *The Letters of Evelyn Underhill*, ed. Williams, pp. 182, 317.

13. Carl Jung, *Psychology and Religion: West and East* (London and Henley: Routledge and Kegan Paul, 1969), p. 214.

14. Robert A. Johnson, *Balancing Heaven and Earth* (New York: HarperSanFrancisco, 1998), p. 196.

15. Anon, quoted by Olive Wyon in *Prayer* (London and Glasgow: Collins Fontana, 1962), p. 98.

16. Adapted from Colin Hodgetts, *Exploring Worship* (London and Oxford: Mowbray, 1980), p. 10.

17. Adapted from Betsy Caprio and Thomas M. Hedberg, *Coming Home: A Manual for Spiritual Direction* (New York and Mahwah

NJ: Paulist Press, 1986), pp. 37–8.

18. Colin Hodgetts' reworking of the collect 'Almighty God from whom all hearts ...' in *Exploring Worship*, p. 64.

19. I have followed Hodgetts' prayer outline (adapted), *Exploring Worship*, p. 64.

20. Taken from Caprio and Hedberg, *Coming Home*, p. 22.

Chapter 8 The third step of love: 'We love God for himself'

1. Etienne Gilson, *The Mystical Theology of St Bernard* (London: Sheed and Ward, 1940), p. 88.

2. St Bernard, *St Bernard of Clairvaux: Selected Spiritual Writings*, ed. M. Basil Pennington (Hyde Park NY: New City Press, 1997), pp. 74–5.

3. Gerard W. Hughes, *Walk to Jerusalem* (London: Darton, Longman and Todd, 1991), p. 131.

4. Raissa Maritain, *Raissa's Journal*, presented by Jacques Maritain (Albany NY: Magi Books Inc., 1974), p. 19.

5. Judith Suther, *Raissa Maritain: Pilgrim, Poet, Exile* (New York: Fordham University Press, 1990), p. 25.

6. Raissa Maritain, *Raissa's Journal*, p. 152.

Chapter 9 The third question: 'Do you know what I have done to you?'

1. Joel Giallanza CSC, 'Three questions for the spiritual journey', *Ministry of Spiritual Direction* (1979), p. 48.

2. *The Letters of Evelyn Underhill*, ed. Charles Williams (London: Longmans, Green and Co., 1943), pp. 51, 64.

3. Elizabeth Gray Vining, *Rufus Jones, Friend of Life* (London: Michael Joseph, 1959), p. 204.

4. Baron Friedrich von Hügel, quoted in Margaret Cropper, *Evelyn Underhill* (London: Longmans, Green and Co., 1958), p. 151.

5. Thomas Merton, *The Seven Storey Mountain* (New York: Harcourt, Brace and Co., 1948), pp. 353–4.

6. Abbé Henri de Tourville, *Letters of Direction* (Harrisburg PA: Morehouse Publishing, 1939 and 2001), p. 72.

7. Carl Jung, *Psychology and Religion: West and East* (London and Henley: Routledge and Kegan Paul, 1969), pp. 155, 157.

8. Eckhart Tolle, *The Journey into Yourself* (Eckhart Teachings Inc., 2003).

9. Robert A. Johnson, *Balancing Heaven and Earth* (New York: HarperSanFrancisco, 1998), p. 192.

10. Etty Hillesum, *An Interrupted Life: The Diaries and Letters of Etty Hillesum 1941–43* (London: Persephone Books Ltd, 1999), pp. 156, 184, 193, 197, 200.

11. Rosemary Hartill in *Our Childhood Pattern*, ed. Monica Furlong (London: Mowbray, 1995), p. 70.

12. George Appleton, *The Practice of Prayer* (London and Oxford: Mowbray, 1980), p. 76.

13. Prayer by Thomas à Kempis (source unknown).

14. Abbé Henri de Tourville, *Letters of Direction*, pp. 61, 66.

Chapter 10 From the third step of love to the fourth

1. Thomas Merton, *The Last of the Fathers* (London: The Catholic Book Club, 1954), p. 85.

2. Section on 'Mary' in William H. Shannon, Christine M. Bochen and Patrick F. O'Connell (eds), *The Thomas Merton Encyclopedia* (Maryknoll NY: Orbis Books, 2002), p. 286.

3. Jean-Pierre de Caussade, *Self-Abandonment to Divine Providence* (London: Collins Fontana, 1971), p. 31.

4. de Caussade, *Self-Abandonment*, p. 38.

5. Eckhart Tolle, *The Power of Now* (London: Hodder and Stoughton, 2001), p. 171.

6. Brother Lawrence, *The Practice of the Presence of God* (London: Hodder and Stoughton, 1981), pp. 19, 23, 73, 75.

7. Brother Lawrence, *The Practice*, pp. 68–70.

8. Raissa Maritain, *Raissa's Journal*, presented by Jacques Maritain (Albany NY: Magi Books Inc., 1974), pp. 57, 48, 61.

9. Bede Griffiths, *The Golden String* (London: Collins Fount, 1979), pp. 184-5, 117.

10. Laurence Freeman, *Jesus: The Teacher Within* (New York and London: Continuum, 2000), p. 245.

11. Thomas Merton, *The Courage for Truth: The Letters of Thomas Merton* (San Diego, New York, London: Harcourt Brace and

Co., 1993), p. 39.

12. Abbé Henri de Tourville, *Letters of Direction* (Harrisburg PA: Morehouse Publishing, 1939 and 2001), p. 18.

13. Jean Sulivan, *Morning Light* (New York and Mahwah NJ: Paulist Press, 1988), pp. 44-5.

14. Eckhart Tolle, *Realising the Power of Now* (British Columbia retreat CD recording, 2002).

15. Kate Turkington, *There's More to Life than Surface* (England: Penguin Books, 1998), pp. 270, 277.

16. Freeman, *Jesus*, p. 244.

Chapter 11 The fourth step of love: 'We love ourselves for God's sake'

1. St Bernard, *St Bernard of Clairvaux: Selected Spiritual Writings*, ed. M. Basil Pennington (Hyde Park NY: New City Press, 1997), pp. 75, 77.

2. Etienne Gilson, *The Mystical Theology of St Bernard* (London: Sheed and Ward, 1940), p. 117.

3. Thomas Merton, *The Last of the Fathers* (London: The Catholic Book Club, 1954), p. 52.

4. Gilson, *Mystical Theology*, p. 88.

5. *Quaker Faith and Practice: The Book of Christian Discipline of the Yearly Meeting of the Religious Society of Friends* (1994), 21.58.

6. Dorothee Soelle, *The Silent Cry* (Minneapolis: Fortress Press, 2001), p. 149.

7. Etty Hillesum, *An Interrupted Life: The Diaries and Letters of Etty Hillesum 1941-43* (London: Persephone Books Ltd, 1999), pp. 356, 395.

8. Dietrich Bonhoeffer, quoted by Soelle, *The Silent Cry*, p. 152.

9. Raissa Maritain, *Raissa's Journal*, presented by Jacques Maritain (Albany NY: Magi Books Inc., 1974), p. 5.

10. Raissa Maritain, *Raissa's Journal*, pp. 373-5.

11. Judith Suther, *Raissa Maritain: Pilgrim, Poet, Exile* (New York: Fordham University Press, 1990), p. 89.

12. A. M. Allchin, *The Gift of Theology: The Trinitarian Vision of Ann Griffiths and Elizabeth of Dijon* (Fairacres, Oxford: SLG Press, 2005), pp. 17, 33, 22.

13. Martin Israel, *Precarious Living* (London and New York:

Continuum, 1976), p. 154.

14. C. S. Lewis, *Surprised by Joy* (London: HarperCollins, 1998), p. 175.

15. Simone Weil, *Waiting for God* (New York: Putnam and Sons, reprinted by HarperCollins, 1951), pp. 88, 90.

16. Michael Mayne, *A Year Lost and Found* (London: Darton, Longman and Todd, 1987), p. 69.

Chapter 12 The fourth question: 'For whom are you looking?'

1. Laurence Freeman, *Jesus: The Teacher Within* (New York and London: Continuum, 2001), pp. 199, 236, 200.

2. Thomas Merton, quoted in William H. Shannon, Christine M. Bochen and Patrick F. O'Connell (eds), *The Thomas Merton Encyclopedia* (Maryknoll NY: Orbis Books, 2002), p. 80.

3. Thomas Merton, quoted in *The Thomas Merton Encyclopedia*, p. 107.

4. Thomas Merton, *The Other Side of the Mountain* (New York: HarperSanFrancisco, 1998), pp. 278-9, 281.

5. Gerard W. Hughes, *Walk to Jerusalem* (London: Darton, Longman and Todd, 1991), p. 93.

6. Mircea Eliade, *No Souvenirs Journal 1957-1969* (London and Henley: Routledge and Kegan Paul, 1978), p. 191.

7. Thomas Merton, quoted in *The Thomas Merton Encyclopedia*, p. 419.

8. Thomas Merton, *Conjectures of a Guilty Bystander* (Tunbridge Wells, Kent: Burns and Oates, 1995), pp. 151, 158.

9. Carl Jung, *Memories, Dreams and Reflections* (Glasgow: Collins Fount Paperback, 1961), p. 346.

10. *Quaker Faith and Practice: The Book of Christian Discipline of the Yearly Meeting of the Religious Society of Friends* (1994), 21.54.

11. James Alison, 'The strangeness of this passivity', *The Merton Journal*, Vol. 10, No. 1 (2003), p. 5.

12. Mark Allen and Ruth Burrows, *Letters on Prayer* (London: Sheed and Ward 1999), p. 6.

13. John Main, *Word into Silence* (London: Darton, Longman and Todd, 1980), p. 53.

14. Thomas Merton, *Thoughts in Solitude* (Boston: Shambala, 1993), p. 89.

15. Charles de Foucauld, 'Meditations of a hermit', quoted in *A Time to Reflect*, comp. Henry Morgan (Oxford: Lion Publishing, 1998), p. 105.

INDEX

➤◄